Alternatives to Capitalism in the 21st Century

Series Editors: **Lara Monticelli**, Copenhagen Business School and **Torsten Geelan**, University of Copenhagen

---

Debates about the future of capitalism demonstrate the urgent need to envision and enact alternatives that can help tackle the multiple intertwined crises that societies are currently facing. This ground-breaking series advances the international, comparative and interdisciplinary study of capitalism and its alternatives in the 21st Century.

Forthcoming in the series:

Money Commons
Remaking Money for an Inclusive and Sustainable Future
By **Ester Barinaga**

Out now in the series:

From Capital to Commons
Exploring the Promise of a World beyond Capitalism
By **Hannes Gerhardt**

Alternative Societies
For a Pluralist Socialism
By **Luke Martell**

Politics of the Gift
Towards a Convivial Society
By **Frank Adloff**

Find out more at

bristoluniversitypress.co.uk/
alternatives-to-capitalism-in-the-21st-century

Alternatives to Capitalism in the 21st Century

Series Editors: **Lara Monticelli**, Copenhagen Business School and **Torsten Geelan**, University of Copenhagen

---

Advisory board:

Find out more at

bristoluniversitypress.co.uk/
alternatives-to-capitalism-in-the-21st-century

PREFIGURING UTOPIA

The Auroville Experiment

Suryamayi Aswini Clarence-Smith

BRISTOL
UNIVERSITY
PRESS

First published in Great Britain in 2023 by

Bristol University Press
University of Bristol
1–9 Old Park Hill
Bristol
BS2 8BB
UK
t: +44 (0)117 374 6645
e: bup-info@bristol.ac.uk

Details of international sales and distribution partners are available at bristoluniversitypress.co.uk

British Library Cataloguing in Publication Data
A catalogue record for this book is available from the British Library

ISBN 978-1-5292-3078-9 hardcover
ISBN 978-1-5292-3079-6 ePub
ISBN 978-1-5292-3080-2 ePdf

Cover design: Liam Roberts Design
Front cover image: 'Hibiscus' by Zualidro
Bristol University Press use environmentally responsible print partners.
Printed and bound in Great Britain by CPI Group (UK) Ltd, Croydon, CR0 4YY

FSC
www.fsc.org
MIX
Paper | Supporting
responsible forestry
FSC® C013604

For Auroville,
and to my fellow Aurovilians.

'The Spirit of Auroville', painted in 1966 by Huta

Contents

List of Figures and Tables

Figures

Table

Glossary

Auroville Foundation   Autonomous body under the Ministry of Education, comprising the International Advisory Council (IAC), the Governing Board (GB) and the Residents' Assembly (RA), represented by its Working Committee (WCom).

Auroville Foundation Office (AVFO)   Office of the Secretary to the Governing Board of the Auroville Foundation.

Auroville Town Development Council (ATDC)   Auroville 'working group' responsible for the planning of the Auroville township.

Budget Coordination Committee (BCC)   Responsible for the management of Auroville's municipal budget, a subgroup of the Funds and Assets Management Committee.

Funds and Assets Management Committee (FAMC)   Auroville 'working group' responsible for the management of the funds and assets of the Auroville Foundation.

Governing Board (GB)   One of the three statutory bodies of the Auroville Foundation, consisting of seven members nominated by the Ministry of Education of the central government of India.

International Advisory Council (IAC)   One of the three statutory bodies of the Auroville Foundation, consisting of five members nominated by the Ministry of Education of the central government of India.

Maintenance	Stipend for Aurovilians.
Pour Tous Distribution Center (PTDC)	Auroville's communal, cooperative grocery.
Residents' Assembly (RA)	One of the three statutory authorities of the Auroville Foundation, composed of all Aurovilians over 18.
Residents' Assembly decision (RAD)	An official decision of the Auroville Residents' Assembly.
Residents' Assembly Service (RAS)	A service that coordinates the decision-making activities of the Residents' Assembly.
Selection process	The Auroville Residents' Assembly's selection process for the members of Auroville's 'working groups'.
Working Committee (WCom)	Auroville 'working group' representing the Residents' Assembly of the Auroville Foundation.
Working groups	Administrative groups and committees of (and selected by) the Auroville Residents' Assembly in charge of the management and coordination of various aspects of community life.

About the Author

Suryamayi Aswini Clarence-Smith is a scholar, activist and educator based in Auroville, India, the largest intentional community in the world, where she is affiliated with the Sri Aurobindo Institute of International Educational Research. Her research on utopian and prefigurative practice is published in the *Ralahine Utopian Studies* series (Peter Lang), the *Alternatives to Capitalism in the 21st Century* series (Bristol University Press) and the *Antipode Book Series* (Wiley). She lectures internationally in academic and activist settings, and facilitates research projects on Auroville as a founding member of the Auroville Research Platform. Suryamayi holds a PhD in International Development from the University of Sussex and a BA in Interdisciplinary Studies from the University of California, Berkeley.

Acknowledgements

I am grateful to all the many Aurovilians who I interviewed and discussed my research with over the years – especially my parents, for whom many a Sunday lunch, innocuous cup of tea or family holiday became occasions for intensive questioning and conversations about Auroville. This research would not have been possible without the trust of Auroville's working groups – each one I asked welcomed my presence at their internal meetings, and I thank them for this openness.

This book is based on my doctoral thesis, undertaken at the University of Sussex, and I would like to appreciate my supervisors, Jon Mitchell and Ben Rogaly, and three other members of faculty, Luke Martell, Geert de Neve and Raminder Kaur Kahlon, for having supported me in this project, as well as Aster Patel at the Sri Aurobindo Centre for Indian Studies (Auroville), Audrey Richard at the French Institute in Pondicherry, Harini Sampath at the Social Research Centre (Auroville), Gilles Guigan at the Auroville Archives and fellow Aurovilians Jean-Yves Lung, Carel Thieme and Maël Vidal who reviewed early work.

I thank Lara Monticelli and Torsten Geelan, the editors of the Alternatives to Capitalism in the 21st century series at Bristol University Press, for supporting the further project of publishing this research as a book, as well as the Sri Aurobindo Institute for International Educational Research and my Aurovilian friend and colleague Henrike Prudon. I hope this work will serve the Auroville community and its ideals, from which it originates.

Foreword

Bem Le Hunte

A society dedicated to a poet, imagined by a mystic and occupied by visionaries is an ideal site for any anthropologist or storyteller. A utopian community exploring the extraordinary possible will undoubtedly also attract revolutionaries and innovators fascinated by Auroville's radical experiment in lived human unity. As an anthropologist, novelist and change maker, Auroville has occupied a central role in my personal journey. Some places have a lasting impact on our being, on our ideals and on the way we live and think. Auroville has had this profound impact on me since my first encounter in 1989. I arrived young and curious, my Indian grandmother's envoy, carrying her wish for me to visit this spiritual community – which she called 'Mother's Dream', after her guru. I walked the red dirt that is often evoked by Auroville's early pioneers (impossibly hard to imagine now while walking through Auroville's fertile forests), and I was taken to the top of a concrete staircase that would later become the Matrimandir, the spiritual centre or 'soul' of Auroville. Sitting high on that plateau with a warm breeze against my skin, I closed my eyes and meditated on a vision for a better world.

Jump forward to 2017 and the Matrimandir is complete. I am visiting on a university sabbatical, welcomed by the remarkable Dr Aster Patel, an early Auroville pioneer and my uncle's cousin (interviewed in this book). It was Aster who introduced me to Suryamayi as one of Auroville's leading young researchers. At the time, she was writing her PhD thesis, which has led to the publication of this intriguing book. I had so many questions and was filled with wonder. How did Auroville work? What did Auroville have to teach the world? I was utterly fascinated by the idea of a utopia designed to promote spiritual and social evolution simultaneously. I delightedly explored the sustainability start-ups that Auroville had engendered. I was particularly intrigued with how a society that aspired to live without money could operate. As someone leading a degree in creative intelligence, I also wanted to understand how innovation and radical creativity worked outside the Western paradigm, and I wanted to know how the young ones were raised because I was creating my own curriculum for 'Being', not just 'Knowing' – described as '21st-century skills' by some.

I have since brought undergraduate students from Sydney to Auroville on global studios to explore these curiosities with me and experience an integral form of learning – learning for whole being. This immersion was repeatedly described as 'life-changing', and every time I returned with student groups, my questions became louder: 'How can we share and upscale the transformative impulse that Auroville embodies for the rest of the world?'; and 'How can we better understand the enabling conditions for transformation so needed in our times?'

Prefiguring Utopia: The Auroville Experiment reveals just how that 'Dream' was made possible. Suryamayi explores so many important questions about Auroville's economic, political and social life in a way that satisfied my anthropological curiosity, while telling stories that spark the fascination of my inner novelist, introducing me to people I have never met and systems that I never knew existed in a tangible way. She also tells her own story through the beautiful and evocative lens of autoethnography, with an acutely honest insider perspective – honest about disappointments, as well as true to the inspiration that she lives and breathes as an Aurovilian who was raised on the soil of transformation. This autoethnographic approach not only matches Auroville's provocative agenda to conduct both inner and outer research simultaneously – 'taking advantage of all discoveries from without and from within' (a line from *The Auroville Charter* [The Mother, 1968]) – but also gives us such rich insights into what it means to grow up in this 'utopian' environment.

While being rich and rewarding in its narrative content, this work boldly embraces scholarly analysis and argument, making it a brilliant and singular contribution to the theoretical understanding of utopias, one in which Suryamayi's love for the subject matter is ever present, as is her own commitment to the experiment. She takes care to contribute to a futures anthropology, describing how the Auroville experiment is not predetermined but constantly adapting – fired as it is by experimentation. She explains the notion of a 'prefigurative utopia' as a work in progress, and this is important, as a 'predetermined utopia' is easy to dismiss when goals are not reached. The idea of a prefigurative utopia that Suryamayi puts forth (so elegantly) helps us to see the work of Auroville as ongoing, through the lens of applied hope and constant emergence – focusing on 'perfectibility, rather than perfection'. Certainly, the ethnographic evidence she gathers through her critical observations and interviews reveal an environment of constant change – from a time when early pioneers started up shared bank accounts with 30 or more individuals to create their own economic collective, right through to Auroville's current system of 'Maintenance', which works much like a universal basic income. Even more valuable, through her study of these experiments and innovations, we learn to understand some of the answers to one residing question from our earliest philosophers: 'How then shall we live?': with a constant thirst for progress, one that is emboldened by the spiritual aspirations of and for humankind.

In her autoethnographic introspection, Suryamayi shares that she felt called to do her PhD, and we have to be grateful that she heard that call. This contribution makes the important work she and her community do accessible and actionable in a time of eco-social crisis when the world is crying out for more creative solutions to the many challenges that Auroville was destined to tackle. The transformative research community needs this study of utopias. With an agenda of transformation, a book on how that transformation actually takes place is both useful and important. While building on the work of radical intellectuals, Suryamayi's work clearly reveals that she too can be counted among their kind.

All Life is Yoga: An Introduction

1968: another world is possible

> Auroville is ...
> A prayer and a curse,
> A suspicious sidelong glance,
> An explosion of silent love;
> A temple in the sun,
> A fractured broken jar,
> A whisper in the wind;
> A laughter and a song,
> A strong fraternal clasp,
> A blasphemy of the Gods.
> A golden-bodied truth,
> A prayer beyond the stars,
> A battlefield of bliss.
> A child against the sun
> A bird against the sky,
> A golden thought unsung
> A flame that is a cry:
> Towards an unknown earth
> That in our hearts does rest,
> And slowly comes to birth
> Breaking slowly forth.
>
> R. Harris, 'Forecomers, Auroville', 1978[1]

In 1968, young people throughout Europe and North America insisted that 'Another world is possible' and sought to claim and enact it. The spirit and culture of this revolution were, in part, informed by the concurrent popularization of Indian spirituality – forever immortalized in the Beatles' 1968 song, 'Across the Universe' – which offered tools for individual emancipation that were seen as necessary to accompany and realize the transformation sought for society at large. In the years leading up to 1968, in India, two 'spiritual activists' had begun (r)evolutionizing the yoga tradition (Flores, 2009). Sri Aurobindo (1872–1950) was a revolutionary in India's independence movement who had turned to spirituality to further the work of realizing an emancipated society, while The Mother (1878–1973) was a French mystic who first met Aurobindo in 1914 in Puducherry, a French colony at the time.[2] Rather than individual enlightenment achieved through ascetic withdrawal, the premise of their 'Integral Yoga' was the spiritualization of all aspects not only of self but also of society.

Auroville was founded in Tamil Nadu, South India, in 1968 by The Mother as an experimental township dedicated to this endeavour. The project drew both young Westerners stirred by the radical period of 1968, seeking alternative ways of living, and young Indian and foreign members of the Sri Aurobindo Ashram, where The Mother resided, in nearby Pondicherry (see Figure 1.1). Some local Tamilians integrated the community with their families from surrounding villages and even further afield, a growing trend in more recent years.

My father, who joined Auroville in 1975, was one of the young protestors of the late 1960s and early 1970s barricading the streets of London. However, unlike his friends at the time, who were focused on 'the revolution' (another famous slogan of 1968 was 'Une seule solution, la revolution' ['Only one solution, the revolution!']), his burning question was: 'What are we going to do once we win it?' In Auroville, he found the answer: a work in progress towards a new society. Janaka, who arrived in 1969 as part of a caravan that left France for Auroville, recalls:

> It was about a month after the Americans had taken their first steps on the moon, they were trying to see if they could change humanity by going to the moon, and well, as for us, we also thought we would change humanity by coming to Auroville to join this experience, and for 50 years we've been in the process, actually. (Auroville Arts Service, 2019)

Aster Patel, an Indian graduate of the Sri Aurobindo Ashram International Centre of Education, Pondicherry, was a student at the Sorbonne in Paris at the heart of the students' revolt in May 1968. The Mother showed a keen interest in the latter, asking Aster to write to her about its developments. When Aster completed her doctorate in philosophy on Sri Aurobindo – on 28 February 1970, two years after Auroville's founding – she returned to the Sri Aurobindo Ashram, where she had grown up. The Mother asked her to work in Auroville, and Aster is an active member of the community to this day.[3]

Figure 1.1: Auroville landscape in the early years

Source: Dominique Darr (Auroville Archives).

Gandhimatti[4] arrived in 1972 with her parents as a six-year-old Tamil girl from the town of Tindivanam. Her father had simply intended to come find work as a labourer, but the family joined the community as Aurovilians in 1975.[5] Gandhimatti was raised and educated in Auroville, where she continues to live and work. "I still do my service for The Mother, like my parents did, I am sure", she tells me, brightly and candidly.[6] My mother was her French teacher; her son and I are the same age and went to school together. Today, we both live and work in Auroville, volunteering together on one of Auroville's committees.

More than 50 years after its founding and Auroville is the largest, most diverse and among the longest-standing intentional communities in the world, with more than 3,300 members of 60 nationalities, approximately half of which are Indian citizens (Auroville, 2022a). Some people have lived in Auroville for all 50 or so years; others joined in the early years and left to return 30 or 40 years later; some born in the community left to study and then returned; and people of all ages continue joining to this day (see Figure 1.2).

This is significant given that there are few similar communities who have lasted and grown over time, as the vast majority are considerably smaller in size and short-lived: 80 per cent do not last longer than two years (Reinhalther, 2014). Auroville is also unique in its breadth of activity: while

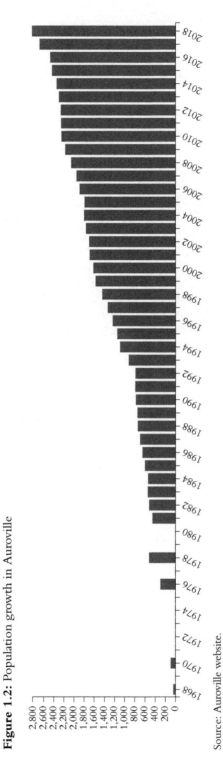

Figure 1.2: Population growth in Auroville

Source: Auroville website.

4

other contemporary intentional communities typically have a more limited or specific set of aims, be these environmental, economic, educational or spiritual, Auroville strives towards a new paradigm of society in which 'all life is yoga' (Sri Aurobindo, 1999: 8).[7] Under this aspirational aegis, a multiplicity of pursuits are undertaken by individual community members, from art to engineering, and innovative and alternative forms and practices at the communal level are developed – for example, of governance, economics and education.

This wide aim and scope of practice has led Auroville to be endorsed and funded by the government of India, the United Nations Educational, Scientific and Cultural Organization (UNESCO) and other international governmental and non-governmental bodies who consider Auroville to be pioneering a model human society, collaborating with: India's Ministry of Education, Ministry of Environment, Ministry of Science and Technology, and Ministry of Non-Conventional Energy Sources; the Indian Renewable Energy Development Agency and the Pondicherry and Tamil Nadu governments; and the European Commission, European Union, United Nations Development Programme and United Nations Centre for Human Settlements (Auroville Media Liaison, 2022). Such embeddedness and recognition within the public sphere are exceptional among intentional communities,[8] with some having faced moral and legal persecution.[9] That said, central government authorities have increased their involvement in the Auroville community since July 2021, following the appointment of a new secretary to the Auroville Foundation[10] who is a member of India's Hindu nationalist party (the Bharatiya Janata Party [BJP]), which is currently in power. This involvement has taken the form of an aggressive drive to accelerate the development of Auroville, which community members argue is in disregard of environmental concerns, as well as their right to take part in defining the future of the community. Some assume that this sudden change in how the government engages with Auroville is linked to the BJP's recent (mis)appropriation of Sri Aurobindo as a Hindu nationalist emblem. Lawsuits filed by Auroville residents in an attempt to restore an equitable balance of power between government authorities and the community are ongoing, as must be the assessment of the risks and benefits of government support for such experiments.

Auroville's development to date is not insignificant. The township, located in the state of Tamil Nadu, a few kilometres from the Indian coastal town of Puducherry, is situated on a plateau that has been ecologically restored and afforested since the community's pioneering years. Its afforestation project is unique: the restoration of the almost-lost rare forest type of the endemic tropical dry evergreen forest, a project recently captured in the award-winning documentary film *Ever Slow Green* (Pohl, 2020). Current infrastructure includes residential settlements, schools, libraries, sports facilities, health and healing arts centres, multimedia performance venues and exhibition spaces, community canteens, restaurants and cafes, small- to medium-scale (predominantly crafts) industries, institutes for scientific and educational research, a town hall and visitors centre, and, at the centre of the community, the Matrimandir, an architectural and landscaping edifice dedicated to spiritual concentration (see Figure 1.3). These have been built with various sources of funding: the personal funds of Aurovilians, money earned by the community's enterprises, and private and institutional donors, including the government of India, European Commission and the Foundation for World Education.

This city area (the central zone of Auroville) is surrounded by a green belt of farms, forest, ecological centres and botanical gardens. Auroville's town plan projects a city of 50,000 permanent residents, occupying a circular area of about 20 square kilometres, and the community currently owns close to 90 per cent of its designated city area and 30 per cent of its designated green belt, with its land holdings being interspersed primarily with private agricultural land (traditionally owned by local Tamilians, some of whom are also members of the Auroville community), temple land and *peramboke* ('government-owned') land (Auroville Media Liaison, 2022).

Auroville's apparent 'success' in terms of longevity, diversity and development is perhaps all the more relevant when considering its challenges.

Figure 1.3: The Matrimandir, Auroville

Ph. Fred Cebron

Source: Photo courtesy of Fred Cebron.

Utopian projects have long been criticized for not being of much relevance to the world precisely because they fail to engage with the challenges that beleaguer it – which include not only practical challenges like food and water security, or societal challenges like economic and political organization, but also challenges of the human condition, both psychological and interrelational. I personally had a positive experience of growing up in Auroville, though, like all places, it has its shortcomings, and challenges that I became far more aware of as an adult engaged in community affairs. A few months after returning, at age 28, from a decade spent abroad, I remember sharing with my high-school mentor that "I never imagined that, all along, it was this challenging for you adults to create the charmed environment we grew up in." I remember being confronted with attitudes and practices that I found shocking in light of my expectations of ours being a community of conscious individuals with a shared ideal of human unity. This was no easy process, and it is one that is shared by other returnees and those newly joining the community. It is probably inevitable for the unseasoned idealist and a trapping of any project with utopian aspirations.

In its 50-year history, the community has known severe economic hardship and experiences of marginalization, cases of suicide and sexual abuse, and violent incidents and threats, both within the fabric of the community and in its interaction with other individuals and institutions – notably, local landowners and politicians, as well as the Sri Aurobindo Society, a legal body under which the community was initially registered and later gained its independence from (see Kapur, 2021). However, unlike many previous historical attempts at creating so-called 'utopian' communities – which sought to enact predetermined, theoretically perfect societies and invariably failed to do so – The Mother conceived of Auroville as an evolutionary experiment. The heart of this experiment would be to collectively embody a spiritualized society, one that could only be progressively discovered and developed through a collective yoga, an applied practice (The Mother, 2003a). Unlike other spiritual communities, such as ashrams, which operate in retreat from everyday life, this would be an experiment in actively transforming society through the spiritualization of its aims, activities and relationships.

Gifts: an outline

As early as 1973, Dr Margaret Mead (1973a) wrote that Auroville deserved 'at least narrative records of what is happening' given the community's dedication to 'working on process in an attempt to develop living forms, both external architectural and environmental forms, and internal styles of human relations, which will transcend our present level of community living which is fraught with such heavy penalties to human beings and to the global environment'. This book will explore how Auroville's spiritually 'prefigurative' practice of utopianism is enabled, challenged and sustained, with insights that I hope will be relevant for the social reproduction of other collectives engaged in embodying a 'pluriverse' of alternative futures to late-stage capitalism (Kaul et al, 2022). Gaining such insights was uniquely accessible to me as both a researcher and a member of the Auroville community, and I hope this work will also serve a purpose for Auroville. As the late David Graeber (2004: 12) said:

> [O]ne obvious role for a radical intellectual is ... to look at those who are creating viable alternatives, try to figure out what might be the larger implications of what they are (already) doing, and then offer those ideas back, not as prescriptions, but as contributions, possibilities – as gifts ... such a project would actually have two aspects, or moments if you like: one ethnographic, one utopian, suspended in constant dialogue.

In Part I, 'Culture', we will begin with a chapter that offers possible answers to the question, 'What is Auroville?', situating the project within the historical and contemporary context of the intentional community movement, the Indian tradition of spiritual communities (or 'ashrams'), the legal framework of India and India's postcolonial context. The second chapter is an exploration of Auroville's unique experimentation with a spiritually prefigurative utopianism in various fields, such as work, art, education and urban design – a contribution to further utopian scholarship that radically reconceptualizes the 'utopian' as dynamic, critically engaged and transformative of present conditions. It also contributes to the scholarship on 'prefiguration', which examines the practice of embodying in the present the attitudes, practices and forms of organizing envisioned for the future.

In Part II, 'Polis', we will turn to Auroville's political life. The first chapter will explore the community's ideals and development as a polity, uncovering a flexible practice of institutionalization that is able to retain a prefigurative nature, while responding to the challenges of scale and social reproduction. Following this, we will delve into an autoethnographic chapter dedicated to a collective decision-making process in Auroville in order to highlight the challenges and potentials of spiritually prefigurative politics. Auroville's collective economic organization and experimentation will be examined in PART III, 'Economy', with a first chapter revealing the legal, financial and administrative challenges of prefiguring an alternative economy, and how the community's founding economic ideals have and continue to underpin this process, while a second chapter will trace a series of experiments in common accounts that have been key to shaping alternative economic organizations within Auroville, affirming the potential of experimental practices for prefiguring alternative models. Each part of the book is split into two chapters: the first providing the overarching cultural, political or economic context of Auroville; the second focused on illustrating and examining how various cultural, political or economic practices play out in order to allow the reader to immerse themselves and gain insight into the lived experience of Auroville.

Emphasis in my research is placed not on the documentation of the alternative practices of the Auroville community, a common focus of intentional community research (see Brown, 2002; Pitzer, 1997; Sargisson and Sargent, 2004), but on why and how these emerge and are established, processes that remain largely under-explored. I believe that turning our attention to the latter is key to understanding whether and how intentional communities are engaged in a prefigurative practice of utopianism, as well as its transferability to other societal contexts. I consider this to be the most theoretically and practically relevant contribution that could be gained from studying them; what research on intentional communities reveals is that there is no uniform set of practices that produces a successful utopian community outcome. On the contrary, existing work highlights the vast diversity of practices that emerge in communities to suit their unique sets of needs and how these inevitably change throughout their lifespans (Pitzer, 1997).

While the most established of intentional communities – Auroville, Findhorn and Damanhur – have each attracted researchers in a variety of fields, from environmental to religious,[11] intentional community scholarship also remains insular because it often fails to connect the practices it examines in these micro-societies with comparable ones exercised in wider social contexts, to consider how they enrich theorizations of the latter and to provide relevant practical insights.[12] As such, it does not significantly contribute to an understanding of the process and potential of societal change inspired by utopian aspirations.[13] Where I do highlight specific practices in Auroville, for example, of horizontal decision making, I relate these to comparable ones adopted in other contexts than intentional communities, in this case, international social movements. I hope that doing so can serve to extend the theoretical scope and contribution of intentional community scholarship in general, as I think there is something we can learn from these laboratories of social change. Whether this can translate into prefiguring change at a larger scale remains an important question, one that other scholars have started to answer (Martell, 2022).

Crucial for yielding insights into the animating processes of intentional community practices are insider understandings, perceptions and experiences of community life and its dynamics. To date, however, individual subjectivity is largely absent from or under-analysed in intentional community scholarship. In my work, I leverage my personal experience and positionality as a member of the Auroville community, actively including these unexplored subjective dimensions to yield a richer analysis of the experience of engaging in utopian practice in the context of an intentional community. I am inspired to do so given the compelling personal experience of being involved in one since my birth and comparative experiences of living in four other countries as a child, teenager and adult. I am fascinated by the alternative values, ways of being and organizing that were fostered in Auroville, as well as the commitment of its members to perpetuating this societal experiment, which I have personally found to be immensely enriching, despite and in the midst of its challenges.

Research: Karma Yoga

Linda Tuhiwai Smith (2012) affirms that native research has a mandate to ground itself in its own, so-called 'alternative' ontologies and epistemologies – ways of knowing, understanding and interpreting ourselves and the world – and thereby honour these. Auroville's founder, The Mother, gave a central place to research in this experimental township. Out of the four points of *The Auroville Charter*, two make reference to it: 'Auroville will be a site of material and spiritual researches for a living embodiment of an actual human unity'; and 'Auroville wants to be the bridge between the past and the future. Taking advantage of all discoveries from without and from within, Auroville will boldly spring towards future realisations' (The Mother, 1968). Auroville's mandate, in essence, is to practically research into – in other words, prefigure – an integral transformation of society across fields, connecting inner and outer dimensions of life. In its first 50 years, animated by this vision, the community has established a basis of applied experimentation in a number of key domains: artistic, cultural, social, economic, environmental, educational and spiritual.

'Research' in Auroville thus has its own endemic conceptualization, closely tied to the community's ideals and to prefigurative practice inspired by these. In 2016, a group of us circulated a survey titled, 'What is research in the context of Auroville?' (Clarence-Smith et al, 2016), through which we sought to arrive at an improved understanding of how research and experimentation are currently understood and undertaken in the community. This was especially revelatory of the perceived, prefiguratively utopian role and nature of research in Auroville:

Research is, in a way, the evolutionary method for Auroville – the way by which it is meant to grow and awaken and evolve. ... It is a place for experiments of all kinds, on all levels and layers of existence and consciousness. In a way, research could simply be another word for Yoga if done in the right Spirit and with a Sincere Will to Grow and become more Conscious. (Participant response to the survey 'What is research in the context of Auroville?', quoted in Clarence-Smith et al, 2016)

The practice of research in Auroville by Aurovilians is diverse, encompassing academic, applied, action and subjective research, with the latter category comprehending a broad range of spiritual inquiry that individuals and collectives perform towards prefiguratively embodying Auroville's ideals in a number of fields. Forms of research include scientific studies, from the restoration of the tropical dry evergreen forest undertaken by the community (Blanchflower, 2005) to the political life of the community (Vidal, 2018; Clarence-Smith, 2019a) and its social psychology (Mohanty, 2008). Examples of applied research include the design of sustainable architectural models for human habitat (such as the award-winning residential project Humanscapes), the elaboration of alternative collective economic models for Auroville to experiment with (see Auroville Radio, 2017a) and the development of transformational educational modalities (such as the community's flagship Integral Yoga programme, Awareness Through the Body[14]). Action research is commonly undertaken in the sphere of Auroville's political life, in which community decision-making processes are constantly being reformulated based on participant feedback, or in education, such as the Learning from the Intangible project, where students and facilitators were involved in assessing an ongoing experiment in Integral Education in their learning centre (Berggreen-Clausen, 2020; Silver, 2022). The arts are a key space of subjective, embodied research and inquiry, notably, into the creation of art inspired by spiritual themes, such as in the annual weeklong Auroville Art Camp.[15]

Professor Emeritus Heidi Watts, who has mentored educational practice in Auroville for the past 30 years, highlights the emphasis on experimental research in the community, which she terms 'research with a small r' ('an attempt to try out something new, to test a theory, an idea, a product and approach'), contrasting with formal research, that is, 'Research with a big R' ('which is what happens when that test is subjected to certain clearly defined boundaries and restraints: limits as to time, place, experimenter, scope, range and variables') (Watts, 2003: 15).

While some in Auroville see the value of 'Research with a big R' for assessing and communicating the applied and embodied experimentation that is happening in the community, others are critical of academic research. They consider it to be dissociated from life and thus ineffectual in its transformational potential, being unable to read and value the spiritual underpinnings of the project of Auroville and, by extension, its research practice. My own intentions and approach to the research I undertook were rooted in my own spiritual experience and practice of Integral Yoga; this process is revelatory of the spiritual experiences of Aurovilians that reflect and inform our world view.

Among the difficult academic arguments indigenous scholars have to make, Tuhiwai Smith (2012) underscores, is that indigenous knowledge is a body of world knowledge that has a contribution to make in institutions and disciplines – in the face of the monoculturalism of Western institutions of knowledge, which prevents the inclusion or consideration of other ways of knowing and understanding. As Angela Cheater (1987: 173) states:

> Continuing verities such as ethnicity and witchcraft cannot be handled – as in Western textbooks – as if both teacher and student were non-believers … we are confronted here by the issue of equality: the necessity to afford the conceptual frameworks of one's fellow-citizens not merely the status of rationality (as limited and closed systems that are ultimately wrong), but also that of an equal and alternative reality that affects oneself.

I will not take on the task of making that argument here for the spiritual dimension of this autoethnographic research but simply offer my experience as an affirmation of, and insight into, it.

"So, where are you from?", asked my undergraduate thesis supervisor at the University of California, Berkeley during our first meeting. I responded tentatively with a one-liner about being brought up in Auroville. Bob was fascinated. He kept asking questions, from personal ones like, "How did your parents meet?", to general ones like, "What form of governance do you practise?" After about 40 minutes of this, I started glancing apologetically through the doorway to the other students who were waiting, each of us scheduled for ten-minute slots. "Well", he concluded, "this is what you will write your thesis on." I was flabbergasted. I could do academic research on Auroville – on my own home? "Is that a legitimate thesis topic?", I asked to assure myself I had heard him correctly. "Of course!", he said, his eyes earnest behind big bushy eyebrows, "It's a PhD!" I was a little overwhelmed. I did not quite take him seriously. Yet it turned out that my thesis (Clarence-Smith, 2015) was awarded highest honours by the department, and several other professors pulled me aside, advising me to take this work into a PhD. However, my first priority was returning to Auroville. I needed to reconnect with my spiritual home and community, and then feel into whether the PhD was what I felt 'called' to do – another very Aurovilian practice of personal decision making. As part of that exploration, I worked on a couple of research projects: one on the Pour Tous Distribution Centre (PTDC), Auroville's communal cooperative (Clarence-Smith, 2016); and one on education in Auroville (Clarence-Smith et al, 2016). I found these incredibly enriching, as they involved deep conversations with fellow Aurovilians that revealed the shared, underlying spiritual dimension that individuals draw from in their everyday life and that fuels our community. More than once, I felt a profound sense of connection with The Mother, Auroville's founder (see Figure 1.4), when I sat down at my desk to write up my research, a

Figure 1.4: The Mother

Source: Anonymous photographer (Auroville Archives).

feeling that she was guiding me to do this work – something I had never experienced before and that so many Aurovilians spoke of (Pommerening, 2017). At some level, I resented that the obvious next step was to pursue a PhD on Auroville. I had just returned, after years of intending to, and did not want to leave again. I also did not think of a PhD as a useful endeavour at all. What would *four* additional years of academic pursuit concretely offer the world? However, there was an undeniable feeling that I was being called to, and I decided to surrender to that, albeit uncomfortably.

Surrendering to the Divine Consciousness – in this case, personified as The Mother – is a key practice of Integral Yoga. It has none of the connotations of passivity that we would associate with the word 'surrender' in a 'Western' understanding, being exercised within a spiritual discipline of action, or work, 'Karma Yoga'. Karma Yoga is one of the three paths of yoga, according to Vedic scripture. It is elucidated in *The Bhagavad Gita*, a foundational text for Sri Aurobindo's philosophy and practice, on which he commented extensively (see Sri Aurobindo, 2015). Essentially, the path of Karma Yoga involves carrying out the work we are being asked to do by the Divine, even if there is something else we could do better, or feel better about, as an act of service and in a spirit of offering to the Divine, and without being attached to the fruits of our action.

The 'gifts' shared in this book are the fruit of my doctoral research, undertaken in Auroville during 2017–18 as part of my PhD in Development Studies. As this research is on my own community, it is autoethnographic in nature. I wished to undertake this research as closely as possible as a community member, instead of as a 'researcher'. I felt that this was something that I could uniquely do as an Aurovilian; any researcher could conduct interviews, but very few could participate in community life in the way that I could. It was this grass-roots experience that I wished to capture, and participant observation was evidently the most appropriate research method for this. While the depth of individual experiences is easily accessible through narrative methods, which are commonly used in research on Auroville (see Devin, 2008), within our community itself, we struggle to understand how we are embodying our ideals at a collective level. The latter is often a source of frustration, disappointment and distrust; therefore, I began by hosting focus-group discussions in which I asked participants what they felt would be the most important aspects of our community to explore. These discussions defined the key areas of focus of my research – economics and governance – which are also central to this book.

My research is also autoethnographic in a second sense of the term, in that I intentionally integrate my own personal experience of undertaking this research, from fieldwork to analysis. I believe that this is valuable because I am a product of the society I am researching – Auroville is a physical, social and spiritual community in which I was born and raised, and with which I have enduring personal ties and involvement – and doing so will perforce be revelatory of attitudes and values fostered in the Auroville context. Some are critical of utilizing and exposing such reflexivity because the traditional ethnographer is mostly invisible (Anderson, 2006), their impersonality serving to promote the research endeavour as objective and scientific (Okely, 1992).

However, it is imperative to understand that such a positionality has its origins in the colonial history of anthropology and that the associated 'pretext of objectivity' (Dumont, quoted in Okely, 1992: 15) has been challenged by numerous ethnographers (Davies, 2007; Okely, 1996). Our own inherent biases as individuals cannot be stripped from the process or production of research; as Okely (1996: 28) states, 'the specificity and individuality of the observer are ever present'. In the face of undeniable subjectivity, reflexivity becomes nothing short of an ethical necessity. The fact that 'the ethnographer's personal history plays a significant role in enabling or inhibiting certain kinds of analytic insights or oversights' (Voloder, 2008: 34) is true of any researcher, not only a native one (effectively debunking the criticism that autoethnographers cannot conduct research on their own communities on the basis that they are subjective – as if the subjectivity of an external researcher were non-existent, as if they did not observe, inquire, relate, analyse and communicate through the lenses of their own backgrounds and experiences).

Some argue that an insider is incapable of having as critical a lens as an outsider because they cannot be objective in their analysis. In *Decolonizing Methodologies*, Linda Tuhiwai Smith (2012: 42) problematizes this bias in favour of external researchers, arguing that it stems from the dominant, rational-objective frames of reference of what she refers to as the 'Western' academy. While insiders may be prone to oversight or a degree of denial due to overfamiliarity and identification with their community, this cannot be juxtaposed against an unchallenged superiority of the research that can be conducted by an outsider.

Exposing a reflexive ethnographic process allows for the 'situating' of knowledge (Okely, 1992), which I consider to be both more ethical and more insightful than upholding a 'pretext of objectivity' (Dumont, quoted in Okely, 1992: 15). Where I fall short of acknowledging my own biases and oversights – something I am especially wary of the potential for as an autoethnographer – I hope that the methodology itself will inherently afford readers the opportunity to become aware of them and that practising such 'self-consciousness' (Cohen, 1992) allows for greater accountability in this regard.

The practice of being reflexive can be a strenuous process, both psychologically and emotionally, and autoethnography is reputed to be a uniquely demanding and trying methodology, prone to difficult self-questioning (Cohen, 1992). Research on one's own community may challenge foundational personal understandings and reframe the nature of the researcher's relationship with their community. In some ways, I was primed for this because both introspection and a questioning of established social practices forms part of the Aurovilian culture. The biggest challenge I could have faced at a personal level was being confronted with realities within our community that violated my understanding of it and were previously unknown to me. I had already undergone a process of being destabilized in my self-understanding of our community upon returning to Auroville as an adult, and I had been able to ground myself into a deeper, more mature and more centred comprehension of it. Auroville also has a culture of adopting a broad view of situations, based on the understanding that an evolutionary process of consciousness is one that is uneven, sometimes seemingly contradictory, conflictual and challenging at both individual and collective levels; this created a basis from which I was able to maintain, or at least return to, a centred, non-reactive and peaceful state. As a result, I was experientially, and not just intellectually, prepared for such challenges to arise in the course of my doctoral fieldwork – which, of course, they did – and to access a subjective objectivity when this was the case.

An unexpectedly enriching experience offered through the research process is one that native anthropologist Stella Mascarenhas-Keyes (1987: 181) describes as having to become a 'multiple native', that is, to transcend one's own pre-existing personal relationship with the community in order to relate with a broader spectrum of community members. For me, this being compelled to become a 'multiple native' was an interesting experience in overcoming what were often unconsciously inherited perceptions about others within the community and even led to new relationships that may not have been formed otherwise. It sparked deeply insightful and revelatory conversations with friends, family and acquaintances that may never have been initiated otherwise. Chang (2008: 54) has highlighted that among the singular benefits of the autoethnographic mode is an increasing sensitivity towards the experiences, positionality and needs of others, potentially even correcting misunderstandings and misperceptions that might be blocking effective responsiveness to communal and interpersonal challenges. Those ethnographers who advocate for reflexivity maintain that it is imperative to do so because it serves to 'situate' knowledge and that this serves a fundamentally ethical function (Okely, 1992). I found that my autoethnographic endeavour allowed me to situate myself, in a reflexive and evolving process, in relationship to my community. I hope this autoethnographic research on Auroville will serve to yield such gifts to members of the community as well.

PART I

Culture

2

Auroville Is ...

Introduction

> If it were a gesture? It would be to open the hands, in a gesture of
> giving, as if to say 'we don't know', as if to say 'nothing belongs to me'.
>
> Khare and Devin, 2012

Tell Me, My Friend, What Is This Auroville? is a book for children by
Aurovilians Jyoti Khare and Christine Devin, in which a small blue rabbit
asks the titular question of the Banyan tree located at Auroville's centre. 'One
cannot answer your question just like that', answers the Banyan; 'You have
to find out for yourself. I can only help you' (Khare and Devin, 2012). The
rabbit decides to try to guess, asking the Banyan a series of questions: what
would it be if it were a wild creature? Or a battle? Or a gesture?

I personally understand and experience Auroville to be a unique spiritual
and societal project embraced and developed by diverse peoples who have
made of it their home, their family, their work and their *sadhana* ('spiritual
path'). However, there are many layers to understanding the community
and many labels ascribed to it from within and without. Is it an ecovillage,
a model township, a cult, a utopia, a neocolonial enclave or a government
project? The Internet is rife with videos made by visiting bloggers who
seem to have found the answer in two days, while researchers and native
authors have offered more nuanced accounts (Minor, 1999; Pillai 2005;
Jouhki, 2006; Meier, 2006; Majumdar, 2017; Kapur, 2018, 2021; Horassius,
2021). In this chapter, I will not seek to define, but rather explore, how
Auroville might be understood through various lenses and how well it sits
in various frameworks.

Establishing communities in which to experiment with alternative ways
of living than in dominant cultures and societies is a diverse and thriving
phenomenon with a long and rich history and scholarship to draw from.
In order to best contextualize the experience of Auroville, I will draw
special attention to other communities inspired by utopian ideals and

Indian spirituality, and that governments have been involved in establishing or supporting. I will also examine Auroville's roots in the Indian ashram tradition and how it is distinct from an ashram and other guru-centric organizations and communities, as well as its recalcitrant assimilation into the ecovillage movement and its uncomfortable embeddedness in a postcolonial context. This exploration will ultimately lead us to an understanding of the prefigurative lens I have adopted for theorizing and understanding Auroville's practice, and why.

Is Auroville an intentional community, hippie commune or ecovillage?

> At a certain stage it might be necessary to follow the age-long device of the separate community ... in which the consciousness of the individual might concentrate on its evolution in surroundings where all was turned and centered towards the one endeavor and, next to formulate and develop the new life ... in this prepared spiritual atmosphere. (Sri Aurobindo, 1970: 1061–2)

Lyman Tower Sargent (2010: 9) defines 'intentional community', an umbrella term that encompasses the vast array of historical and contemporary communal experiments,[1] as: 'A group of five or more adults and their children, if any, who come from more than one nuclear family and who have chosen to live together to enhance their shared values or for some other mutually agreed upon purpose.' Such communities have come into existence for many different reasons and taken various forms throughout history. They have been religious, spiritual and secular in nature. They include groups that are strongly bounded, such as monastic orders, and others that are open, such as educational communities. Some aspire to be institutionally complete, developing their own educational, economic and governmental institutions; others, such as co-housing cooperatives, arise to fulfil a specific socio-economic need. Although the majority are established in rural areas, they exist in urban settings too: co-housing cooperatives are a common feature of such major cities as London and San Francisco – Christiana, a commune situated within the city of Copenhagen, is among the largest in the world. They include anarchist communes and ones planned by governments. While, by and large, intentional communities have been critiqued as escapist, insular, indoctrinating and incapable of perpetuating themselves, they have also attracted recognition for their radical attempts to reinvent society and for pioneering progressive practices that were later adopted into mainstream society (Bouvard, 1975; Schehr, 1997).

The earliest known forms of intentional communities are religious and spiritual in nature. Buddhism and Christianity both have an extant monastic tradition dating back at least 2,000 years. Sanskrit, perhaps the world's most ancient (Indian) language, has a specific word for spiritual communities, 'sangha', and India has a living legacy of 'ashrams', spiritual residential communes, which today exist throughout the world. The first recorded account of a communitarian 'movement' seeking benefits other than religious or spiritual seclusion is found in St Paul's 5th-century letters, describing a wave of communitarianism among Christians who sought political and cultural freedoms within the enclave of community living.

That these early communitarians sought out not only religious freedoms but also those relating to aspects of public and social life demonstrates that communitarianism as a device for the pursuit of alternative and – at least by internal understandings – progressive lifestyles has historical antecedents distinct from religious and monastic forms. Given that the nature of the Auroville project is one that is socially reformist according to spiritual ideals and practice, it is also important to note that social change was sought among, and enacted by, religious peoples in creating these separate communities; as we shall see, this is a continuous trend in the history of intentional communities.

According to the online community directory of the Foundation for Intentional Community,[2] there are thousands of intentional communities in existence throughout the world today, encompassing such a wide variety of aims and arrangements that contemporary scholars warn against generalization and even comparison (Sargisson and Sargent, 2004). Let us therefore begin by looking at the three most successful intentional communities – in terms of size, longevity and recognition – that are active today. Findhorn is an international, ecological, educational community founded in Scotland by a charismatic female mystic in 1962 focused on sustainable living, made up of approximately 400 members from 40 different countries; it has been awarded the UN Habitat Best Practice designation, and regularly hosts sustainability seminars in affiliation with the United Nations Institute for Training and Research (Findhorn Foundation, no date).

The spiritual and artistic community of Damanhur, founded in 1972 in Italy, has a current population of approximately 600, primarily comprised of Italians; it has also received a UN Global Human Settlements award for sustainable communities (Damanhur Foundation, no date). Auroville, significantly larger, with a population of 3,300, has been recognized by UNESCO in five of its resolutions – in 1966, 1968, 1970, 2007 and 2017 – for its contributions to the advancement of innovative and sustainable, peaceful and harmonious social, cultural and educational development (Auroville, 2022b). It is also recognized and funded by the Indian government as a registered foundation under its Ministry of Education (see Auroville, 2020a; 2022c).

All three of these communities are exceptional in the breadth of their activities; each experiment with alternative forms of governance, economic and ecological practices, and have their own educational institutions and health centres. Auroville appears to be the most developed in terms of an autonomous alternative society, perhaps by virtue of its size. Creating institutionally complete communities, however, was not a determining feature of contemporary 'hippie communes' formed in the 1960s and 1970s primarily in the US, as well as in New Zealand and Australia and across Europe and the UK. These were inspired by the celebration of emancipatory social relations in the wake of the civil rights and feminist movements, conscious protest as part of the anti-war movement, and the growing awareness of environmentalism (Bouvard, 1975; Schehr, 1997). Many incorporated elements of Indian spiritual philosophy and practices, popularized in the West at the time, into their alternative lifestyles, and these drew young, international seekers to India, some of whom joined the Auroville community in its early years, alongside members of the Sri Aurobindo Ashram and the local Tamil population.

Environmentally friendly lifestyles have been a growing concern of intentional communities since humankind's negative impact on the living planet became understood and popularized, notably, through Rachel Carson's (1962) *Silent Spring*. The term 'ecovillage' came into use in 1995 with the founding of the Global Ecovillage Network, an organization that promotes the visibility of communities that experiment with various dimensions of sustainability – ecological being a key focus – in an effort to catalyse a global shift in lifestyles (Global Ecovillage Network, no date).

Auroville is celebrated for its environmental restoration of the plateau on which it is situated through afforestation and water conservation, to which its pioneering years were primarily dedicated. The community also uses renewable energy sources, sustainable building techniques and natural cleaning products, and engages in a culture of upcycling. Many feel that we have a long way to go before being able to claim that we are an 'environmentally friendly community', which is one reason why some Aurovilians reject the term 'ecovillage'. The more fundamental reason, however, is that Aurovilians understand the community's primary aim to be a spiritual transformation and all other aims, including ecological ones, to emerge from this primary catalyst of change (Pommerening, 2017). There is also the explicit goal of Auroville becoming a city of 50,000 and wanting to be understood as such a project in the making, despite the fact that its currently population (at 3,300) is that of a village. This is singular in the landscape of intentional communities – many remain small because they have no intention to scale (and therefore no motivation to summon the financial and human resources to do so). The slogan 'think global, act local' captures the value they see in establishing 'sustainable' microcosms in which harmonious face-to-face human relationships and ecologically low-impact living can be demonstrated. While for some community members, the goal of achieving a city is pursued purely because that is what The Mother envisaged and it therefore has a spiritual significance or promise, it is also argued that achieving a sustainable city would be more relevant to advancing the goal of environmentally friendly lifestyles than remaining the size of a village, no matter how eco-friendly, given that the majority of the world's population lives in urban settings and these require a comparable alternative model (Majumdar, 2018). Although there are environmental, social, economic and organizational concerns among Aurovilians in terms of how, how fast and to what extent scaling up is to be undertaken, there is therefore nonetheless a widespread understanding that doing so is important if Auroville is to provide a relevant, replicable model for a township that is sustainable in each of these areas.

Is Auroville a 'utopian' community?

A map of the world that does not include Utopia is not worth even glancing at, for it leaves out the one country at which Humanity is always landing. And when Humanity lands there, it looks out, and, seeing a better country, sets sail. Progress is the realisation of Utopias. (Wilde, 1891)

Intentional communities are often understood as 'utopian' projects, though this framing is contentious for many, from academics to intentional community members themselves. This is largely because of the dominant identification of the concept of utopia with a fixed ideal of perfection, which many intentional community members feel that they are far from, and its association with a detailed, predetermined blueprint, towards which much sound criticism has been levelled (Kateb, 1963; Sargent, 2010). These associations are not without basis, but they are, by and large, outdated. The first so-called 'utopian' communities were established in the 19th century and were indeed largely based on blueprints provided by utopian social theorists and writers, such as Robert Owen, Charles Fourier and Henri Saint-Simon (Bouvard, 1975; Schehr, 1997) (see Figure 2.1). Often, these were accompanied by city plans that would create the settings for such societies to be organized within. The perfectly planned city as the means to realizing the ideal society later became a project espoused by urban planners – in the 1950s, when The Mother first began imagining Auroville, the most famous contemporary project being Brasilia.

While these 19th-century communities were the product of an intellectual elite and attracted a significant number of educated, cultivated and well-respected individuals – politicians, scientists, academics, social reformers and educators – their practice was often derided and threatened, both by law and by local communities who considered them to be deviant. Under

Figure 2.1: New Harmony, a utopian attempt, depicted as proposed by Robert Owen

Source: Engraving by F. Bate, London, 1838.

various combinations of external and internal pressures, most disbanded, disintegrated or changed form, and were thus considered to be failures.

How we evaluate the success and failure of intentional communities was problematized as early as 1972 in Rosabeth Kanter's (1972) sociological study, *Commitment and Community*. Kanter proposed a number of measures of success for such communal experiments, such as whether the community satisfied its members during the time it was active, which are of continued relevance in assessing these communities today. Contemporary utopian scholars maintain that the perception of the failure or inadequacy of these communal experiments has its root in the 'mistaken reading of utopias as perfection-seeking, blueprinting and desirous of perfection and finality' (Sargisson, 2000: 11). Thomas Moore coined the term 'utopia' by combining the Greek words for 'good place' ('ou'-topos) and 'no place' ('eu'-topos), the implication being that utopia is an unattainable ideal, painting attempts to reach it as naive (Sargent, 2010).

Over the last several decades, however, there has been a radical move away from the idea of utopia as synonymous with perfection, fixity and the intangible, and towards the dynamic articulation of a utopian aspiration within, and seeking alternatives to, present 'mainstream' conditions – or perfectibility, rather than perfection (Sargent, 2010). The concept of what could constitute a utopia became internally diverse and changeable, imperfect, reflexive and self-critical in terms of form and content (Moylan, 1986; Sargisson 2000; Levitas, 2011a). Thus reformulated, 'utopian' better reflects the practice and experience of contemporary intentional communities, Auroville among them. Based on her research in Findhorn,

Sargisson (2000: 3) emphasizes that these are not based on, nor do they construct, 'a blueprint for the ideal polity'; on the contrary, there is 'no full-stop to the process of politics in this utopianism. ... It is, above all, resistant to closure and it celebrates process over product' (Sargisson, 2000: 3).

Auroville is not an entirely non-prescriptive utopian endeavour, in that it does have founding ideals and even a model for a city plan, determined by a founding figure who was recognized as a spiritual guru. While there was no strictly specified societal 'blueprint' for Auroville to realize, The Mother (1954) did draft *A Dream* in 1954, which envisioned an ideal society. She also wrote a short, four-point charter for the community, *The Auroville Charter* in 1968, and a guiding document for individual members, *To Be a True Aurovilian*, in 1970 (The Mother, 1968, 1971). The intentional absence of a defined approach to realizing Auroville's ideals and exhortation that Auroville be a place of research has fostered a plural and experimental environment that seeks to prefigure these ideals. While The Mother did make specific provisos for certain aspects of the community's collective organization, notably, in the sphere of economy, whether and how these now historical statements should be applied and evaluated in the community's current context is frequently questioned. There is a trend of using specific statements made by The Mother regarding Auroville during its founding years to lend authority to certain views and projects, including opposing agendas. Notably, the community's leading archivist has pointed out that even within the short period in which The Mother was actively envisioning Auroville, her statements on the community's purpose demonstrate a significant evolution in conceptualization over time (Guigan, 2018).

According to the Marxist utopian philosopher Ernst Bloch (1986), the utopian function is to continually reach into the 'Not-Yet-Become', and that it is precisely against a 'finished aspect' of static perfection that the utopian must 'prove its worth' (Bloch, 1986: 172). This evolutionary dimension and function of the utopian is congruent with Auroville's ontological framework of Integral Yoga, which seeks to hasten the spiritual evolution of consciousness through an applied embodiment in the present. So too does Bloch's (1986: 223) insistence that utopian ideals must be connected to potential embedded in existing reality in order to give rise to 'concrete utopias' that can foster the development of 'tendencies' or 'latencies' existing in the present, no matter how compromised the conditions. The Mother conceived of Auroville as an experiment dedicated to this process and purpose, something that underpins members' self-understandings of the community (see The Mother, 2003a).

Is Auroville some kind of ashram or religious cult?

While Auroville readily lends itself to being understood as part of the intentional community movement and has been recognized by scholars as a secular, albeit spiritual, community (Minor, 1999), it is important to note its roots in the Indian ashram tradition, as well as its point of departure from the latter. India has a long history of ashrams: centres where devotees of a certain spiritual figure or 'guru' gather and often reside alongside them. Traditionally, ashrams were places where *sadhaks* ('spiritual practitioners') renounced and retreated from worldly lives in order to pursue contemplative and devotional practices, such as meditation, study and chanting, under the guidance of the guru, as well as *darshan* (literally, 'viewings'), that is, public or private interactions with the guru.

In the 19th century, the phenomenon of 'guru organizations' (Warrier, 2003a, 2003b) – in which some gurus and their ashrams take on missionary activities related to both spiritual education and humanitarianism, and establish centres internationally – began to emerge. In doing so, some sought to reform society, such as Swami Vivekananda, perhaps the forefather of this practice.[3] The most famous current example of such a 'guru organization' is that of 'the hugging Amma', Mata Amritanandamayi Devi, a female guru from Kerala who has founded numerous charitable organizations and ashrams internationally and engages in worldwide travel (Warrier, 2003a, 2003b).

As already noted, Auroville is closely associated with Sri Aurobindo, one of India's most famous spiritual figures, and his collaborator, The Mother, who founded the Sri Aurobindo Ashram in the late 1920s and Auroville in the late 1960s. The Sri Aurobindo Ashram in Pondicherry (see Figure 2.2) is a different type of spiritual community and endeavour; neither a centre of renunciation nor a missionary organization, the ashram was 'created with another object than that ordinarily common to such institutions, not for the renunciation of the world but as a centre and a field of practice for the evolution of another kind and form of life' (Sri Aurobindo, 2011: 847). There are no set rites or practices for the ashramites to follow; instead, they engage in numerous secular activities of 'ordinary' life, seeking to make them a part of their yoga, or spiritual practice. One of Sri Aurobindo's iconic phrases is 'all life is yoga' (Sri Aurobindo, 1999: 8); all aspects of life were to be imbued with a higher consciousness in 'an effort to create a new life-formation which will exceed the ordinary human society' (Sri Aurobindo, 1970: 1060).

Both anthropological and insider accounts of ashram life are generally lacking. The Sri Aurobindo Ashram stands out in this regard, with two books written by disciples whose object is the life of the ashram itself (Prasad, 1965). Mukherjee's (1997) *Sri Aurobindo Ashram: Its Role, Responsibility and Future Destiny* is a uniquely valuable piece, in that it offers an insider's assessment of the challenges and issues faced in the ashram – something often glossed over in the prevalent hagiographies of gurus, personal accounts of disciples (see Osborne, 1954) or bitter criticisms of ex-members (see Caldwell, 2001).

Figure 2.2: Sri Aurobindo Ashram, Pondicherry

Source: Pinkapani (Wikimedia Commons).

Sri Aurobindo referred to the ashram as 'a first form which our effort has taken, a field in which the preparatory work has to be done' (Sri Aurobindo, 1970: 13). This sheds some background insight as to how and why The Mother came to found Auroville in 1968, as a second 'form' through which to realize Sri Aurobindo's vision of a life divine: an experimental township. While she acted as a managing guru of the Sri Aurobindo Ashram, Auroville was to be a community developed by its own members, with no predetermined organizational structures and rules.[4]

Another Indian guru who explicitly attempted to form a utopian community out of his ashram is Bhagwan Shree Rajneesh, later known as Osho.[5] Born in 1931, he first created an ashram in Pune in 1974. In 1981, Rajneesh and about 2,000 of his followers formed an international, intentional community in Oregon (USA), projected to become a society of 50,000, and obtained the legal status of a city (Urban, 1996). Rajneeshpuram only lasted four years, after which Rajneesh relocated to the old ashram in Pune, which he renamed the Osho Commune International (Goldman, 2009) – today, a spiritual resort (D'Andrea, 2007).

Academic work on Rajneeshpuram and the ashram in Pune emphasizes the hierarchical and coercive nature of the community, as well as and the 'overpowering social control' (Latkin, 1991: 368) effectuated by the community leaders Rajneesh had appointed. Faith in the charismatic

Rajneesh and the desire to remain near him overshadowed doubts regarding contentious community policies, with members remaining silent for fear of being expelled (Latkin, 1991). Not being dependent on a guru for its day-to-day organization, management and development, Auroville has avoided such pitfalls of charismatic leadership, prevalent in both guru-centric ashrams and intentional communities worldwide.

Although Auroville was founded by The Mother, a guru at the head of an Indian ashram, and many Aurovilians refer to records of her intentions and recommendations for the township's development, it is clearly a distinct form of spiritual community to existing Indian ashrams. Aside from their shared basis of Integral Yoga, the kinship between the Sri Aurobindo Ashram and Auroville is perhaps most obvious in the socio-economic organization of the township, something that will be addressed in Chapter 6, as well as their common pedagogical practice of Integral Education, explored in Chapter 3. While Auroville was historically affiliated with the Sri Aurobindo Ashram, located in the neighbouring city of Pondicherry, the community is currently registered as a secular foundation under the Ministry of Education of India's central government and has no ties with the Ashram; these developments are examined in Chapter 4.

The question of whether Auroville is a religious institution or cult has arisen in the community's history and been at the heart of a number of court cases, both foreign and domestic. It was first answered by the Constitution Bench of the Supreme Court of India on 8 November 1982 in a case brought forth by Aurovilians to secure their independence from the Sri Aurobindo Society, who held that Auroville was a religious project and thereby should remain under their purview. The court held that 'there is no room for doubt that neither the Sri Aurobindo Society nor Auroville constitute a religious denomination and that the teachings of Sri Aurobindo only represent his philosophy and not a religion' (Supreme Court of India, 1982: 5). Supreme Court Judge O. Chinnappa Reddy concluded:

> The management of the International Cultural Township of Auroville cannot be said to be a matter of religion. Auroville is a township and not a place of worship. It is a township dedicated not to the practice and propagation of any religious doctrine but to promote international understanding and world peace, surely a secular and not a religious activity. (Supreme Court of India, 1982: 11)

The Sri Aurobindo Society lost the case, resulting in Auroville's registration as a secular foundation. This judgment has since been followed in other countries, notably, France and Germany. In France, a case was filed by a divorcé against his former wife for bringing their children to live in the community and another by parents against their daughter for bringing her children to Auroville, arguing that it was a cult. In Germany, a case was filed against Auroville International Germany on the basis that money donated to this non-profit organization was being routed to a religious organization. In each case, foreign courts concluded that Auroville is not a religious institution or cult.

However, within Auroville itself, there are ongoing concerns around how the figure of The Mother is related to as a spiritual founding figure, specifically, the prevalent display of her (and Sri Aurobindo's) image in public places, as well as practices of invoking her statements in public forums and of wielding views she expressed to support political agendas, which will emerge throughout this book. While Auroville is implicitly and explicitly understood to be a spiritual community, there is a certain wariness around the dangers of dogmatism that may spring from the explicit articulation of the latter; current and historical examples of this are highlighted in Chapter 3.

Is Auroville a government project or neocolonial enclave?

Auroville is clearly not a project conceived by the Indian government, though it should be noted that there is a history of intentional communities being encouraged, established, designed or supported by governments. In the British colonial period, the British government used utopian imaginaries to encourage and incentivize British subjects to form settler colonies, first in the US and later in New Zealand. In the later colonial period, these were actively influenced by the concurrent discourse of utopian socialism (Sargent, 2010). Interestingly, both New Zealand and the US have a rich subsequent history and present-day practice of intentional communities, including ones formed by their governments to address social and economic problems. In the US, this occurred in the context of the Great Depression of the 1930s, where close to 100 communities were constructed as a form of relief and resettlement (Sargent, 2010). In the 1970s, the New Zealand government's Ohu programme attempted to alleviate issues of unemployment and disaffection (particularly among youth) through planned communities (Sargisson and Sargent, 2004). The 20th century also saw the kibbutz movement, among the most important of communitarian movements, being supported by the Israeli government as a model of national development. Interestingly, this finds echoes in the anti-colonial national development that Gandhi sought to foster in India, a socio-economic and political organization based on networks of village communities. Individual communities currently in existence – notably, Auroville, Damanhur and Findhorn – have also garnered governmental and UN support in the form of financing, partnerships and recognition of their innovative potential and practices.

Auroville's registration as an autonomous foundation under a government ministry is singular (the Findhorn Foundation, for example, is registered as a charitable trust) and has prompted the question of whether Auroville is a 'government project'. While the legal structure of the Auroville Foundation recognizes three authorities, two of which are committees appointed by the Ministry of Education, the third is composed of all members of Auroville. The spheres of authority and consultative relationships between these bodies ensure that the latter retains a significant degree of autonomy, which will be looked at in detail in Chapter 4. However, Auroville has recently seen unprecedented government involvement in its development, seemingly as part of a nationwide campaign led by the Hindu nationalist party in power to promote Sri Aurobindo as a national figure for his 150th birth anniversary year (2022–23) and its efforts to promote spiritual tourism in India. Such involvement has been contested by Aurovilians in a number of court cases, the outcomes of which are still pending and will be revelatory of the degree to which the government is able to intervene in the community's life and growth.

Throughout this conflict, some community members have stressed the need to collaborate with the Indian government to ensure the continuity of the project. Meanwhile, a narrative that has been instrumentalized by government authorities is that foreigners have established and wish to protect a sort of neocolonial enclave on Indian land (Namakkal, 2021).

In *A Dream*, The Mother (1954) envisioned 'a place which no nation could claim as its own, where all human beings of goodwill who have a sincere aspiration could live freely as citizens of the world'. While Auroville is the most diverse intentional community in the world –in terms of not only national and cultural backgrounds but also class and caste – the postcolonial context in which it is embedded adds many layers of complex and problematic dynamics to its attempt to embody a multicultural utopia, one in which individuals are able to transcend 'social, moral, cultural, racial and hereditary appearances' and live as 'true Aurovilians' guided by an 'inner discovery' (The Mother, 1971). Recent scholarship has not satisfactorily addressed and unpacked the complexity of Auroville's postcolonial positionality and experience (Namakkal, 2021). As a foreigner born and raised in Auroville with many associated forms of privilege, I am undoubtably prone to oversight when it comes to doing so and likely to be both biased and perceived as biased towards discrediting the critique that Auroville is a neocolonial community. The observations I offer here are done with the objective of revealing a complexity that has so far been overlooked and hopefully informing in–depth, future scholarship on this critical dimension of the Auroville project.

When considering Auroville's early entanglements with the colonial history of the region, it is important to recall that while the community was founded by a French woman who settled in French colonial Pondicherry, she did so in order to support the work of the Indian freedom fighter turned spiritual sage Sri Aurobindo. Sri Aurobindo had settled in Pondicherry – a French enclave – in order to avoid arrest by the British Raj for his revolutionary activities as a leader of India's independence movement. His presence drew a growing number of primarily Indian disciples to the town, including the French Mira Alfassa who first visited Pondicherry in 1914 with her husband, Paul Richard, as he sought election to the French Parliament from the colony. Alfassa eventually formed an ashram around Sri Aurobindo and later the Auroville community, in which utopian aspirations merged with the aims of Integral Yoga. While Auroville attracted more foreigners, also by virtue of the fact that the time period in which it was established (the late 1960s) was one that saw increased travel to India, it also attracted more local Tamilians than the ashram.

Although recent scholarship on the decolonization of French India argues that the early, predominantly foreign demographic presence in Auroville meant that the project enacted a movement of 'settler utopianism', it unfortunately fails to grasp the significant Tamil demographic presence in Auroville (Namakkal, 2021: 3).

One could imagine a neocolonial enclave as a gated community in which foreigners working for the interest of foreign industry, governments or other organizations live separate from a local population. However, today, approximately half the community's population is Indian, which notably includes a range of castes. While Namakkal also argues that the early foreign demographic meant that the project was 'guided by European interests, a way for the privileges of colonial mobility and wealth to continue into the postcolonial world' (2021: 3), foreign residents of Auroville are awarded visas that only allow them to live in, and work for, the community, whose funds and assets – including the houses people have financed and the enterprises they have created – are the legal property of the Auroville Foundation, an Indian entity.

A neocolonial enclave would also be one in which foreigners were able to exert disproportionate power over a local population, arguably through the possession of disproportionate wealth, education and political connections. While there is a vast gulf in economic, educational and social standing between Auroville and its immediate rural surroundings, one that was reflected among members in the early population constellation of primarily middle-class foreigners and rural Tamilians, the lines of privilege today are more complex to draw. Among the members of Auroville are Indians of various castes and classes, hailing from cosmopolitan cities and overseas universities, as well as local villages. Foreign nationals, apparently largely from middle-class backgrounds, have in many cases invested their capital into the community, while being granted residency by the Indian government on the basis of temporary visas. While second- and third-generation foreign Aurovilians have seen family inheritances dwindle, local Tamilian families owning land in the area – particularly Auroville's master plan area – have seen its value exponentially increase. While Auroville employs a large 'working class' of non-Aurovilians, primarily local Tamilian and Nepali workers – which warrants fair criticism in terms of the community perpetuating dynamics of class stratification – it has also fostered the economic development of a previously rural area. Some of its enterprises support women's economic empowerment by exclusively offering work to local women, while a variety of schools and vocational programmes have been set up to serve the local population. That said, postcolonial contexts and dynamics are necessarily flawed and uneven, and targeted research is needed to fully unpack Auroville's role in sustaining or transforming the latter (see Jouhki, 2006).

The community has known underlying tensions and explicit accusations of racial discrimination between community members; however, it should be noted that these have been observed across the fault lines of not only foreign to Indian but also North Indian to South Indian, and even Tamil to Tamil, in which class and caste play an important role – an important dimension that has not been discussed in recent work (Namakkal, 2021). Attempts to address these fault lines remain few (and perhaps for this reason remain unexamined), including a process of cross-cultural dialogue held by the community's Restorative Auroville team and a facilitated forum in which a group of Tamil community members discussed these issues with the Working Committee, that is, Auroville residents' selected representatives. More recently, the stoking of a narrative of sharp division between Aurovilians of foreign and Indian origin (in the context of increased government involvement) has been actively rejected by a younger section of Tamil community members, who responded by organizing meetings and events celebrating the community's unity in diversity, achievements and right to self-governance (*New Indian Express*, 2022).

In short, there are important and ongoing dynamics and tensions that stem from Auroville's predicament of being an international, utopian experiment embedded in a postcolonial Indian context (see Figure 2.3) that harbours its own, innate challenges around inclusion and social equity. Transcending these is a complex and multilayered endeavour. While there are both encouraging and frustrating accounts of how this plays out, it is fair to say that the Auroville community still needs to seriously address challenges around social equity. Recent scholarship (Namakkal, 2021) has not evoked and assessed the agency and interventions of both community members and the local population in this respect, nor been able to do justice to the disjointed, sometimes surprising, ways in which postcolonial privileges are subverted or transformed within the Auroville context. More in-depth interrogation

Figure 2.3: Laughter Day in Auroville

Ph. Marco Saroldi

Source: Marco Saroldi (Auroville Digital Archive).

and analysis, including participatory research methods, might be able assist a transformative agenda of decolonization in Auroville and beyond.

Is Auroville a prefigurative project?

'[T]o prefigure is to anticipate or enact some feature of an "alternative world" in the present' (Yates, 2015: 4), and fittingly, scholars have begun to adopt the concept of prefiguration to describe intentional communities given that they are a radical, embodied exercise in redefining society according to alternative values, both of the present and for the future (Farias, 2017; Monticelli, 2018). The term 'prefigurative' was coined in 1970 by the cultural anthropologist Margaret Mead, an early endorser of the Auroville project, to herald the advent of a newly future-oriented 'prefigurative culture', one in which 'it will be the child – and not the parent and grandparent – that represents what is to come' (Mead, 1973b: 204).[6] While scholarship on prefiguration has been focused on political practice, more recent research ventures into other areas, such as economic, environmental and pedagogical practices (see Mason, 2014; Monticelli, 2022). Few scholars relate prefiguration to utopianism (Juris, 2008; Dinerstein and Deneulin, 2012; Yates, 2015; Monticelli, 2018); however, prefiguration is central to how I understand utopian practice in the Auroville context (Clarence-Smith, 2022) given that the practice of prefiguration is one in which a collective emulates in the present the attitudes, social relations, culture and organization it envisions for the future through 'experimental and experiential' (van de Sande, 2015: 189) means (Maeckelbergh, 2011).

I consider the 'utopianism' conceived and practised in the Auroville context to be spiritually prefigurative, for the premise of the Auroville project is to evolve into a spiritualized society through the transformational practice of informing everyday life and activities with spiritually enlightened ideals, values and consciousness. As we have seen (and will continue to throughout this book), Auroville is a society with many challenges and contradictions. In prefigurative practice, it is understood that 'the struggle and the goal, the real and the ideal, become one in the present' (Maeckelbergh, 2011: 4). It is a practice to be engaged within the limitations of a given present context, with the objective of practically, progressively and ultimately transforming these, just like Bloch's (1986: 223) concept of the utopian was to transform present conditions by drawing forth the potential embedded in present realities. In the coming chapters, we will explore how Auroville engages in a spiritually prefigurative utopianism throughout cultural, political and economic realms of community life and development, while navigating contextual challenges.

3

A Spiritually Prefigurative Culture: The Uniqueness of Auroville's Utopian Practice

Introduction

> Les utopies ne sont souvent que des vérités prématurées. [Utopias are often only premature truths.]
>
> De Prat de Lamartine, 1847: 322

In 1977, the term 'prefiguration' was first used to define 'the embodiment within the political practice of a movement, of those forms of social relations, decision-making, culture, and human experience that are [its] ultimate goal' (Boggs, 1977: 100). The context was the 'New Left' social movements that arose in the 1960s, peaking in 1968 (the year Auroville was founded) with the students' revolt in Paris, which The Mother was very interested in. These protests were precipitated and shaped by changes in culture and lifestyle – captured in the feminist movement's slogan 'the personal is political' – and early scholars of prefiguration conceptualized a broad spectrum of social movement practices as prefigurative (Breines, 1989; Epstein, 1991). In this chapter, we will look at a few examples of how practices in Auroville are uniquely spiritually prefigurative – in realms as diverse as work, art, education and town planning.

Over the last decade, the label 'prefigurative' has risked becoming exclusive to horizontal forms of organizing and decision making in social movements like Occupy Wall Street and the Global Justice Movement (Franks, 2003; Maeckelbergh, 2009; Graeber, 2010). Only such 'strategic' practices, that is, ones that directly engaged with achieving political change, were identified as prefigurative, while the role and significance of sociocultural/lifestyle practices in prefiguring social movements' overarching goals were disregarded (Yates, 2015). The restrictive scope on strategic political practice is perhaps why prefiguration has barely been associated with utopianism (see Juris, 2008; Dinerstein and Deneulin, 2012; Yates, 2015; Monticelli, 2018). Yet, those articulating a prefigurative politics are driven by the desire to live in a radically different society, shaped by alternative values than those of mainstream capitalism, understood not just 'as an economy but as a society' (Streeck, 2016: 201). Such an alternative society needs to be prefigured in all its aspects – education, work, social relations and so on – an exercise that intentional communities engage in through utopian practice.

However, while the utopian practice of such communities is not necessarily tied to political change in mainstream society, prefigurative practice is expected to enact and engender such change. This is upheld even by those who argue that prefiguration can refer either to alternative political mobilization or to alternative everyday practices: '[P]refiguration necessarily combines the experimental creating of "alternatives" within either mobilisation-related or everyday activities, with attempts to ensure their future political relevance' (Yates, 2015: 13). Just like utopian communities, however, prefigurative politics are criticized for being apolitical. Prefigurative social movements are condemned for adopting an 'exodus approach' (Mouffe, 2013: 111) from the public sphere; a common criticism of utopian communities is that they draw energy and activism away from working for social change in mainstream society, and that they are insular and escapist projects.

Yet, activists and scholars of each maintain that they are engaged in the articulation of new and alternative repertoires of social and political organization and practices: 'By their very existence intentional communities broaden the choice of values and institutions for society as a whole, a welcome addition to any democratic society which upholds pluralism' (Bouvard, 1975: 5). Intentional communities are noted as having made little-known but significant contributions to the broader societies in which they are embedded, being harbingers of forward-looking practices born from, and reflective of, progressive values, later to be adopted into the mainstream (Schehr, 1997). These were developed through what was effectively the politicization of their everyday lifestyle practices, leading Sargisson (2000: 74) to remark that their members are to be reconceived as 'active citizens', instead of 'dropouts'. For example, New Harmony, the historical intentional community founded by Robert Owen in Indiana in 1814, is recognized as a pioneer of free public education and free public libraries open to men and women, which have since become US institutions (Schehr, 1997: 28).

Over the last 50 years, Auroville has been a focal point for pioneering innovative forms of collective and economic organization, renewable technologies, sustainable architecture, educational practices, and social enterprises, with award-winning local, regional, national and international reach and impact. For example, the Auroville Earth Institute holds the UNESCO Chair of Earthen Architecture, researching and educating people worldwide in earthen building technologies, while Tamil Nadu state textbooks have recently incorporated educational content on waste

Figure 3.1: Participatory action research in Auroville's Aikiyam Outreach School with Wasteless

Source: Marco Saroldi (Auroville Digital Archives).

management from the Auroville social enterprise Wasteless, reaching millions of Tamil children (Auroville, 2021a; see also Figure 3.1).

I have heard several fellow Aurovilians describe these as simply 'by-products' of the underlying spiritual mission of the community. This active role of spirituality in (re)shaping public life is especially interesting to consider given that a prevalent criticism of spiritual practice is that it renders individuals apolitical (Žižek, 2001; Chari, 2016: 227). It is relevant to note that academic work endorsing this critique is grounded in Buddhist-based practices, such as mindfulness, which emphasize detachment from worldly life – although in recent decades, Buddhist leaders like Thich Nat Hahn have decisively committed their spiritual practice to social, political and environmental activism, a phenomenon that has attracted its own scholarship (see Hahn, 1993; Queen and King, 1996; King, 2009; Queen, 2012). By contrast, the spiritual world view of Integral Yoga is one that sees the world as a realm to be divinized through a practice of cultivating not only 'spiritual consciousness within but also spiritual life without' (Sri Aurobindo, quoted in Mukherjee, 1997: 9), engaging in the pursuits of worldly life with an applied spirituality to participate in transforming these.[1] Following Sri Aurobindo's iconic phrase 'all life is yoga' (Sri Aurobindo, 1999: 8), the Auroville community seeks to engage with all aspects of life in spiritually prefiguring society as a whole. This includes the community's political life, and interestingly, while spiritually inspired practices like moments of silence and meditation have been used in decision-making processes of prefigurative social movements, these have not featured in scholarship on prefiguration per se (see Chari, 2016: 236; Rowe, 2016). Perhaps this is due to the aforementioned focus on 'strategic' prefigurative practices (Yates, 2015) or to a reticence among academics to engage with spiritual ontologies (Morton, 2015).

An open question for scholars of prefiguration is: 'Where does the political begin and end in the case of building alternatives?' (Yates, 2015: 5). In *Utopian Bodies and the Politics of Transgression*, Sargisson (2000: 65) argues that alternative lifestyle practices in intentional communities are 'politicized partly because of their context: the fact that they occur in a consciously created and alternative space ... and also by the consciousness of the actions themselves'. If the aspiration of Aurovilians, as a polity, is an embodied, individual and collective evolution of spiritual consciousness in everyday life, then any activity – a physical discipline, artistic production, political forum and so on – in which they intentionally engage with this spiritually prefigurative process is fundamental to Auroville's development as a spiritual polity. In the following, I will seek to elucidate the spiritually prefigurative nature of Auroville's utopian practice by exploring a variety of 'embodied' aspects of community life, such as education, work and art. In so doing, I will also point to some of the challenges that such prefigurative practice necessarily entails in attempting to embody a more spiritually evolved future within the limitations of a present context. I will then turn to the example of town planning in Auroville, as it is the area in which tensions between a 'predetermined' and 'prefigurative' utopian approach are the most acute in the community, and it is along this fault line that the Auroville community is currently experiencing one of its toughest challenges to date.

The spiritually prefigurative nature of Auroville's utopian practice(s)

Before delving into exploring the spiritually prefigurative nature of Auroville's practices, it is important to note that there are no explicit protocols for individual or collective spiritual development. Nor did The Mother define a fixed blueprint for this alternative society, for she anticipated that this would constrain the community's capacity to develop in accordance with the progressive spiritualization of life, which its members were to consciously participate in. Interestingly, this spiritually anticipatory dimension harks back to the original use of the term 'prefiguration', which has its roots in religion and refers to a prophetic foreshadowing (Raekstad, 2018: 361).

While certain collective aspects of Aurovilian society today – such as political and economic organization and praxis, which we will look at in subsequent chapters – are institutionalized to a certain extent, reformulation is common. This is reflective of the community's overarching experimental and evolutionary ethos and praxis, and echoes the 'inherently experimental and experiential' nature of prefigurative practice (van de Sande, 2015: 189). It is also consistent with Sargisson's (2000: 2) observations of utopian practice in other intentional communities, such as Findhorn, which she describes as 'flexible and resistant to permanence and order'. In the Auroville context, this flexible and open-ended practice, inscribed in the community's founding political ideal, is deliberately designed to serve and respond to a spiritually prefigurative process of evolution. Let us first turn to examples of Auroville's embodied, alternative sociocultural practices and how these engage in this process.

Education

In any society, education is a key site of deliberate social reproduction, and alternative pedagogies have been an important feature of many intentional communities, both historical and contemporary, such as New Harmony and Findhorn. While I will be focusing here on the education of Auroville's children, what has come to light for me in the course of my research is that many aspects of Aurovilian society are shaped in ways that facilitate it being a place of 'unending education' and 'constant progress', as envisioned in *The Auroville Charter* (The Mother, 1968), and that individuals are strongly inspired by these ideals in both personal and community life (Clarence-Smith, 2019a).

As we will see next, work is a key site of lifelong learning in Auroville, our rhizomatic self-governance being a key site of civic education. Engaging in this 'learning society' (Clarence-Smith, 2019b) is also accessible to non-Aurovilians. Educational opportunities are rife in Auroville's wide-ranging 'units' – including farms, architecture studios and social enterprises working on waste management – and hundreds of volunteers from across the world immerse themselves each year in learning within these. Some complete internships as part of their university requirements, notably, Indian architecture students in Auroville's studios. University student groups regularly visit the community with their faculty as part of accredited modules and courses, such as the American University of Paris and the University of Technology Sydney. The community also welcomes long-terms guests, who often engage in the many workshops Aurovilians facilitate, from trainings in earthen building techniques at the Auroville Earth Institute to courses in aquatic bodywork at the Quiet Healing Center.

A study of the *Educational Practices & Opportunities for Adults in Auroville* (Grinnell et al, 2013) reveals that Aurovilian facilitators aspire to embody and transmit 'integral' educational experiences to their participants, drawing on 'discoveries from without and from within', as per *The Auroville Charter* (The Mother, 1968). The study also reveals that being immersed in the broader context of a spiritually conscious society facilitates the accessibility of an inner dimension of learning and transformation. So too does 'Lessons from utopia', a chapter in the *Palgrave Handbook of Learning for Transformation* based on the experience of students participating in a visiting university programme held in Auroville (Le Hunte et al, 2022). As we will see later on, children educated in the community also highlight the significance of embeddedness in this wider 'learning society' context.

The inward directionality of 'unending education' is complemented by an actively outreaching one, which reaches beyond the community. Auroville has several so-called 'outreach schools' that serve children from local villages; in fact, more children are educated in these than there are Auroville kids. Aurovilians have also established centres that provide educational programmes to local youth and women (some reaching further afield) in topics including maths, handicrafts and hatha yoga. Some date back to the early years of Auroville, such as Udavi School, founded in the early 1970s (Udavi School, no date), and Ilaignarkal, an 'anytime school' for local Tamilian employees of Auroville, founded in 1977 (Auroville, 2014). These are financially supported by the community, alongside other schools and educational centres for adults in Auroville, including Savitri Bhavan (a research centre dedicated to the study of the works of Sri Aurobindo), the Auroville library and others (BCC, 2022). A quarter of the municipal budget goes towards education, its most highly funded sector (BCC, 2022); there is also a regular grant from the Indian Ministry of Education for educational research, channelled through the Sri Aurobindo International Institute of Educational Research (SAIIER), established in Auroville in 1984 (Auroville, 2016).

Having breezed through the broader learning context of the community, let us dive into the field of childhood education. Interestingly, a study I collaborated on in 2016, 'Auroville education survey: 1968–2013' (Clarence-Smith and Tewari, 2016), which surveyed alumni of Auroville schools active over a 45-year timespan (the oldest to fill in the survey was born in 1959 and the youngest in 1991), revealed that alumni considered the Auroville upbringing as a whole to be an educational experience, reaching beyond schooling (see also Figure 3.2). Today, Auroville has several primary and secondary schools, where teachers seek to engage and experiment with the pedagogical philosophy of Integral Education based on Integral Yoga and initially developed at the Sri Aurobindo Ashram (Tanmaya, 2014). The premise of Integral Education is to foster a spiritually conscious, values-based, well-rounded and self-directed development of the student; the objective is to form individuals who are aware of both the inner and outer dimensions and potentialities of education, and of the significance of pursuing such personal development throughout their lives.

Integral Education does not have a set curriculum, as this would go against its core mission of fostering 'free progress' guided by the psychic being (or

Figure 3.2: Children at the Auroville Town Hall

Source: Marco Saroldi (Auroville Digital Archives).

soul) of each child. One noteworthy programme developed in Auroville is Awareness Through the Body, 'a practice that assists children and adults to come to better know the complexity of their own being and find ways to manage this complexity more effectively, so as to become more self-directed beings organized around their psychological center, the inmost, truer part of their being' (Awareness Through the Body, 2023). It helps individuals discover the existing connections between mind, emotions and the physical body, and offers ways to bring these parts together in a more harmonious whole through a range of dynamic and introspective exercises in individual, partner and group activities. Awareness Through the Body evolved out of a postural education class that was started in Auroville schools in 1992. '[A] subject to "study oneself"' (Awareness Through the Body, 2023), it has since developed into a comprehensive practice for both children and adults, taught internationally. Auroville students – myself included – single it out as being the most meaningful aspect of their educational curriculum, something captured in a survey of alumni of Auroville schools (Clarence-Smith and Tewari, 2016).

As an overall pedagogy, Integral Education is very much in the process of being discovered, or prefigured, which explains in part its multiple schools, engaging in different approaches. While some schools have been criticized for being experimental to a fault – to the point of being closed down – others are reproached for being too traditional, perpetuating mainstream educational practices, such as preparing students for Indian and international examinations, in order to enable them to easily integrate into higher education institutions.

While the vast majority of alumni who participated in the survey[2] felt that they significantly benefited from their Auroville upbringing, there were some bitter testimonials from students in the early years, during which radical measures like closing down all schools and burning books to give space for the 'free progress' of youth were carried out by radical adult community members (for an account of this period, see Kapur, 2021). The alumni highlighted the lack of training of the teachers, the lack of structure and continuity of educational opportunities, and the lack of guidance for youth in the community:

> I was influenced by adults who had many idealistic views and ideas, some were my teachers. Not being qualified or trained educators they probably had no idea of the influence and impact they had on young impressionable minds ... many years later when I left Auroville I realized a formal education was required to be able to function in life ... one could not but feel a sense of abandonment and even of having been cheated. (Survey respondent, quoted in Clarence-Smith and Tewari, 2016: 16)

While the community's educational sector is well established today, with numerous schools in place, ongoing concerns are harboured by members of this generation around the undesirable aspects of experimentation, even though the latter is recognized as both valuable and central to the community ethos:

> Even though Auroville is an experiment and I agree that there should be a constant search, I feel this can only be done in a very responsible and controlled manner. There have been in Auroville's history too many individuals that have tried out systems and ways of education based on their personal convictions and ideas, often with negative results on the students. (Survey respondent, quoted in Clarence-Smith and Tewari, 2016: 30)

This search for balance between experimentation and stability reflects a broader tension that the community at large has been navigating with a process of flexible institutionalization, notably, in its political and economic organization, which we will turn to in later chapters.

The survey also revealed that a key request was for Auroville to develop internal forms of recognition for the range of educational experiences of youth within the community and to move towards international accreditation for these. In this way, its Integral Educational approach could be upheld, unconditioned by the demands of mainstream institutions, while nonetheless allowing Auroville students to access a university education. Some alumni nevertheless felt that it was important that Auroville's educators engage with other curriculums as a way of both informing and learning from these, again reflecting the intention set out in *The Auroville Charter* to draw on 'discoveries from without and from within' (The Mother, 1968):

> Auroville should be seen to be a leader in child education and there has been a tremendous amount of research and progress in the education of children around the world and, if we follow our charter, we should be keeping abreast with it and incorporating this into our education system, as well as contributing to the body of research. (Survey respondent, quoted in Clarence-Smith and Tewari, 2016: 30)

This question of whether Auroville's seeking recognition from, and engagement with, the mainstream would contribute to the political relevance of its prefigurative practices (for example, through replication in other contexts) or disempower them was reflected in the responses. One individual cautious about the latter stated: 'I do not think Auroville needs to go down that path. There are countless institutions that create recognition certificates for educational levels attained. I think for Auroville it is more important to focus on the inner education and desire to explore it rather than creating recognition on outer forms' (survey respondent, quoted in Clarence-Smith and Tewari, 2016: 28).

Having understood some of the challenges of prefiguring an alternative educational landscape, let us turn to the key question of whether Auroville and its educators have been successful in fostering a spiritually prefigurative milieu. According to survey responses, the vast majority resonate with, aspire towards and strive to embody and practically apply Auroville's spiritual ideals in their daily lives – even those who no longer live in the community:

> I feel that as children of Auroville, we were brought up with the ideas of Auroville and the Charter. What ever much or how ever much we understand from the written context, I believe that we express the Charter or the ideas of Auroville better through our actions in our day-to-day life because it's part of us, it's deeply embedded in us whether we know it or not. (Survey respondent, quoted in Clarence-Smith and Tewari, 2016, 17)

> I connect with them on an everyday basis, whether I am in Auroville or not. ... I carry that atmosphere and those words in me. I try to let that feeling out and I try to express it in my everyday work. I am not a true Aurovilian, I am not sure what that may be, but I work

towards it every day. (Survey respondent, quoted in Clarence-Smith and Tewari, 2016: 18)

The last sentence – 'I am not a true Aurovilian, I am not sure what that may be, but I work towards it every day' – captures the spiritually prefigurative nature of being Aurovilian: anchored in experimental, everyday practice. Its intrinsically utopian nature – in the Blochian sense of utopian as anticipatory and evolutionary – is captured in yet another testimonial: 'I think that the characteristic of an Aurovilian is this sensation of looking towards, to always talk about what can be or what could become' (survey respondent, quoted in Clarence-Smith and Tewari, 2016: 21). Next, we turn to how this spiritually prefigurative process is embodied in other pursuits among adult members of Auroville.

Work, art and personal development

Work in Auroville is another key site for spiritual development, central to the understanding of community life given the founding statement that 'Auroville is for those who want to do the yoga of work' (The Mother, 2003b: 222). This signifies that work is to be undertaken as a yogic practice through which individuals would progress spiritually, while also participating in a transformation of the world by infusing consciousness into their worldly occupations.[3] The focus on 'the yoga of work' arises from ancient Indian Vedic teachings that identify 'Karma Yoga' – the yoga of worldly action – as one of the *margas* ('three paths') of spiritual practice in the yoga tradition.[4] While Karma Yoga is traditionally understood as a practice for the individual to progress spiritually, Sri Aurobindo identified Karma Yoga as central to Integral Yoga because of its potential in fostering the spiritual evolution of existence as a whole. Karma Yoga is a practice of surrendering and offering the focus and outcomes of one's worldly deeds to a higher spiritual power, and, in the context of Integral Yoga, of participating in the transformation of the world through the intentional spiritualization of our worldly pursuits (Sri Aurobindo, 2015).

While it is safe to assume that not all community members are engaged in work that is meaningful to them or that not everyone approaches their work as a spiritual practice, research does show that the ideals and understandings of spiritualized work are actively practised by Aurovilians (Seidlitz, 2016; Pommerening, 2017). This is evidenced as the practice of dedicating one's endeavours to The Mother (understood not as the individual but as the divine presence she embodied), a quest for beauty and perfection in various efforts that seeks to 'divinize' these, and a deep-seated receptivity towards aligning oneself to the work that one is called to do in service of one's own highest purpose and the needs of the community (Seidlitz, 2016). While this may read as highly agreeable, this can translate into taking up work that is not particularly desirable, well remunerated or otherwise gratifying.

As mentioned previously, these observations pertain exclusively to Aurovilian members of the community and not to its non-Aurovilian employees, many of which are socio-economically disadvantaged local Tamilians who engage in manual labour, women notably in handicrafts and food preparation, and men in construction, agriculture or forestry. Given this socio-economic reality, questions are raised around the neocolonial character of the community (Namakkal, 2012), though as explained in Chapter 1, these issues have not yet been adequately examined. Academic research is yet to be done on the various experiences of work in the broader Auroville community, including Aurovilians, volunteers and employees; to date, researchers have focused on social enterprises that exclusively hire local women with the aim of providing them with safe and dignified work, such as Naturellement and Wellpaper, a food confectionary and upcycling operation, respectively (van der Heyden, 2020; Gurkaya, 2018).

Auroville's enterprises confront themselves in multiple ways with a mainstream capitalist market, not only in addressing their labour requirements but also in selling their goods and services. While all are arguably social enterprises, in that their revenue is invested into the alternative community of which they are a part, many cite a variety of aims other than supporting Auroville financially, notably, providing solutions for social and environmental issues (Eveleigh and Arumugam, 2021: 39). One such example is Ecofemme, an organization dedicated to the development and education of ecologically sustainable menstrual hygiene products. Another is Mason & Co, an organic, bean-to-bar vegan chocolate company, which has created a new market in India for this environmentally conscious product. While engaging in market-based activities, such enterprises are nonetheless seeking to influence the Indian marketplace (and beyond) to favour socially and ecologically sustainable practices – and in some cases, succeeding in doing so.

How does the market influence the pursuit of employment in Auroville? As we have seen, engaging in the yoga of work is central to the Aurovilian identity (which by its nature will perpetually be a work in progress). The Mother also spoke of work in Auroville not as 'a way to earn one's living but a way to express oneself and to develop one's capacities and possibilities' (The Mother, 1954). Flexible trajectories of work in the community allow for this personal development; engaging in various fields of community activity over the course of one's involvement is common, including at a given time. This versatility does not typically require any kind of formal qualification or even prior experience. In my experience and observation, interest, commitment and the willingness to learn seem to be of primary importance.

While this accessibility is celebrated for offering individuals opportunities to pursue their interests, it has also led to issues with people who lack competence for chosen work in the 'public sector' of Auroville's community services nevertheless persevering with it, in some cases, to secure their 'Maintenance' (the Auroville stipend). Although the fact that this provides them with an opportunity for self-development is valued by other members of the community, the social and economic cost to the collective of them occupying positions they do not adequately fulfil is also a source of dissatisfaction. Despite this, such situations are often not addressed due to a community culture of reticence in overruling individual members and a lack of human resources in general. The Auroville Maintenance is the same regardless of the nature of work in its 'public sector', though Auroville's income-generating units are able to supplement this financial support, something that can attract Aurovilians to seek employment within these. It is also not uncommon for Aurovilians in financial need to temporarily take up work outside of the community or even in parallel with their community work. When establishing Auroville, The Mother had envisioned an economy in which the basic needs of all would be provided for with no exchange of money (for details, see Chapter 6), in which Aurovilians would not only not be driven to working long hours but also be able to dedicate a significant amount of their time to the integral development of their beings. However, this has not yet been achieved and there are various, ongoing financial pressures on Aurovilians, such as investing in housing and caring for children, notably, the funding of higher education.

That said, many Aurovilians do partake in various avenues of personal development within the community (outside of work), including: physical practices like yoga, tai chi, dance; meditative, contemplative and healing practices; reflective and therapeutic work, such as non-violent communication and family constellations; and artistic production and performance (see Figure 3.3). In keeping with Auroville's economic values, many of these are available to Aurovilians free of cost. Some are financed by the municipal budget or grants from the SAIIER; therapeutic centres, such as Quiet and Vérité, subsidize treatments or classes for Aurovilians with income generated from outside clients; and in some cases, sessions are offered according to the generosity and financial capacity of individual teachers and therapists. This includes not only regular weekly classes but also trainings that enable Aurovilians to become certified aquatic body-workers or Awareness Through the Body facilitators, for instance. Pursuing such opportunities is restricted to the wealthy in the vast majority of modern societies – an hour-long yoga class in the US is almost double the hourly minimum wage. Beyond these personal development opportunities, both the municipal budget and the SAIIER subsidize performances, concerts and art exhibitions, making them free to Aurovilians and visitors to the community – while such cultural exposure is, again, often expensive and thus limited in its accessibility to the general public elsewhere.

Figure 3.3: Co-creating Kolam at the Matrimandir

Source: Marco Saroldi (Auroville Digital Archives).

Auroville's arts scene ranges from rock, pop and jazz bands to visiting Indian classical musicians, and from the tango and Bharatanatyam (a Tamil classical dance form) to contemporary dance performances. Community theatre includes original pieces performed by adults and children, as well as renditions of common plays or ones written by Sri Aurobindo. A significant body of artistic practice and performance is inspired by the literature on Integral Yoga and by the community's ideals. Indeed, art has long played a central role in the utopian imaginary because it offers a space in which to challenge present conventions and envision and embody alternatives. The Burning Man festival, a radical gathering held annually in the ephemeral Black Rock City, constructed for, and disassembled after, the event in the Nevada desert, is perhaps the largest and most popular contemporary collective exercise of this, and also draws significantly on spiritual repertoires (Gilmore, 2010). For the township's 50th anniversary in 2018, Aurovilian artists created multimedia works based on chapters of a key text on Integral Yoga, *On the Way to Supermanhood* (Satprem, 1985), and a theatre group adapted chapters of the same volume for stage performance. The community's ideal of 'human unity – in diversity' (Auroville, 2020b) was symbolized and explored in a multidisciplinary community performance, Soul Encounters for the Auroville Soul, which fused dance forms from various cultures and culminated in a hatha yoga sequence and meditation that represented the epitome of spiritualized embodiment.

The examples just shared reflect how the arts are a space of spiritually prefigurative exploration in Auroville; it is also worth highlighting that the community has an artistic culture of satire that offers many a welcome respite from the high expectations we place upon ourselves: plays, skits, cartoons and videos produced by Aurovilians as a commentary on various aspects of our community have been common and long-standing vehicles through which we reflect on, critique and laugh about ourselves and our society. Such performances as the Auroville Trashion Show, in which community members are invited to create costumes out of trash and sashay down a catwalk, while information is compellingly narrated on the issue of waste generation and disposal, serve to raise awareness on not only local but also global issues (Paitandy, 2019).

Town planning

Having explored aspects of community life in which Aurovilians intentionally engage in prefigurative utopian practice, let us turn to a major dimension of the Auroville project in which a predetermined and prefigurative conception of utopianism come to a clash: town planning. As highlighted in Chapter 2, town plans were a feature of the historical 19th-century 'blueprint' style of utopian communities – ones whose utopian organization, goals and practices were predetermined. Planned cities like Brasilia and Chandigarh were contemporary to the Auroville project, and The Mother envisioned that Auroville would have a specific spatial organization to support the development of the township. She employed French architect Roger Anger to design a novel concept for this novel project. The Mother refused a progression of multiple proposals, the first based on a classical grid structure, until Roger arrived at a dynamic, spiralling Galaxy Model (see Auroville, no date). At the centre was the Matrimandir, 'the soul of the Auroville' (The Mother, 2003b: 223), from which four zones radiated outwards, the whole held by a circular green belt that would serve as a buffer zone between the city and the outside world.

Roger set up an urban design studio in Pondicherry and continued to develop the concept in more and more detail, though it remained a concept and was not developed into a proper master plan. While the Galaxy concept is celebrated by many Aurovilians for the dynamism it embodies, there are also strong criticisms of how it is translated into realities on the ground. Roger himself is recorded as having said:

> Auroville ... should be at the service of those who live there. That means this city will not be constructed first, and then occupied, but it will be the inhabitants who will define by a living experience the needs of the city. This approach is the opposite of that taken up to now by contemporary urban planners. Cities have been built and then people have been asked to inhabit them. Here the problem is reversed. (Klostermann, 1972)

However, there are also testimonials of him asking people to move from settlements made in the early days of Auroville, as he wished to replace them with the specific urban features that he envisioned (see Kapur, 2021). Similar tensions are still alive in Auroville today and have escalated since December 2021, as the new secretary of the Auroville Foundation, appointed by the government of India, has sought the forceful clearing of existing structures and afforested areas to make way for urban development as conceived in a perspective master plan finalized in 2001 (Auroville Foundation, 2001). Residents recall that this plan was designed as a tool to protect the Auroville area from unwanted development and land acquisition by other parties, and argue that it was never intended to impose a specific development agenda onto the Auroville community – the latter even 'guaranteed' in the meeting at which the master plan was approved. The Auroville Foundation Act 1988 maintains that the Residents' Assembly (composed of all Aurovilians) is to 'formulate the master plan of Auroville' (Section 19[c]), while the 'Auroville universal township master plan: perspective 2025' (Auroville Foundation, 2001) document itself has an in-built review process (Section 2.11.1), as well as environmental management processes (Section 2.9.7), and specifically states that it will 'neither be traditional, nor static, nor rigid' (Section 2.11.1).

Those in favour of progressing with development as per the 'Perspective 2025' master plan uphold that Auroville's spatial organization has spiritual significance, notably, the perfectly circular Crown Road it defines around the Matrimandir, which is currently being pursued. Those who adhere to this 'blueprint' articulation of utopian practice (a minority in the community) believe that accomplishing this urban design will propel the spiritual evolution of Auroville (as it is based on the vision of its spiritual founder, The Mother). While this approach also seeks to support the realization of a spiritualized society, its emphasis on achieving a fixed and 'perfect' outcome stands in contrast with the experimentation and flexibility at the heart of prefigurative practice. Furthermore, it provides a clarity and simplicity that a prefigurative approach lacks, something that has likely played into the capacity of a minority group to obtain the support of government authorities.

Others in the community have engaged with a spiritually prefigurative approach to articulating and manifesting the Galaxy through a process called Dream Catching, in which anyone interested in exploring this topic would gather in various places in Auroville at sunrise in 'an atmosphere of receptivity to whichever glimpses of the higher vision wish to emerge' and share any 'subtle insights' received on a given planning theme, following an opening mantra and period of contemplative silence (Nightingale, 2008: 12). The aim was to 'delineate inspiring and uplifting architectural and urban design parameters to lead us inexorably in the direction of building a "yogic" city' in the hope that the Auroville township would 'develop in such a way that it would nurture an increased awareness and consciousness in its inhabitants' (Nightingale, 2008: 12).

Soon a corollary 'sunset session' emerged, in which architects presented proposals to one another for a given project and sought to arrive at a synthesis that would reflect the 'highest common factor', rather than the 'lowest common denominator' (Nightingale, 2008: 13). After a first round of presentations, architects were encouraged to borrow the best ideas of others and 'weave' these into a revised design. This process would continue until a final design (or designs) emerged that could be agreed upon by all.

This original method was successfully used as a design tool for a number of projects in Auroville, such as the Sustainable Livelihood Institute in 2015 and one of the Matrimandir gardens – the Garden of the Unexpected – in 2018. A first process for Dreamweaving the Auroville Crown, 'Crownways', was held in 2008, but its ideas were dismissed by members of Auroville's Town Development Council (L'avenir d'Auroville at the time) because it was designed to avoid non-Auroville land (and, as such, was not perfectly circular). At the height of the conflict following the forced clearing in December 2021, another, larger process of Dreamweaving the Auroville Crown was started, one that I personally participated in organizing. Unlike previous Dreamweaving exercises, the designs of architects were presented to community members for feedback, and their inputs were also taken into account for reworking. Many sought to respond to tensions between realities on the ground and 'Perspective 2025' master plan directives creatively, for example, proposing that the Crown Road transform into a walkway/cycle path in an ecologically sensitive area. The process has been identified as holding potential for developing all aspects of the township informed by the unique sensibilities of residents, reflecting Roger's vision of it being 'the inhabitants who will define by a living experience the needs of the city' (Klosterman, 1972). However, even this effort was viewed as endorsing a departure from the vision of The Mother by those community members who adhere to the urban design blueprint reflected in the master plan. While the process was called for by the secretary of the Auroville Foundation (who ordered the clearing), there has been no commitment to use the outcomes of the Dreamweaving the Auroville Crown 2022 process (Aggarwal et al, 2022) in the urban development of the township – by either the current Auroville Town Development Council (appointed by the secretary of the Auroville Foundation) or the Governing Board (under whose authority the secretary exercises her duties), which is mandated to ensure development as planned in consultation with the Residents' Assembly (Section 17(e) of the Auroville Foundation Act 1988). This conflict around town planning and other misgivings regarding the development of various aspects of the community and how it embodies its values are a strong source of disappointment and internal criticism within the community. Let us turn now to the question of how these tensions impact the utopian practice of the community: do they undermine or sustain it?

The role of hope, disappointment and criticism: sustaining a communal utopian practice

Hope features strongly in the new body of theoretical and ethnographic work on utopian practice, following utopian philosopher Ernst Bloch's (1986) path-breaking work *The Principle of Hope* (Dinerstein and Deneulin, 2012; Dinerstein, 2015; Monticelli, 2018). For Bloch (1986: 3), utopian practice is 'a question of learning hope. Its work does not renounce. … [It] requires people who throw themselves actively into what is becoming, to which they themselves belong.' While hope is certainly a primary driving and sustaining force for a utopian endeavour, from autoethnographic observation and experience, I consider it necessary to add the dimension of disappointment, as I have found this to be key in fostering an ongoing drive for social change within Auroville. I would go so far as to extrapolate that it is the tension between these two forces – hope and disappointment – that engenders the dynamism at the core of grass-roots, concrete utopian practice.

Criticism is a natural ally to disappointment in this dynamic. Tom Moylan, among the contemporary scholars of utopianism, has defined some utopias as 'critical', in both the 'Enlightenment sense of *critique* – that is the expressions of oppositional thought, unveiling, debunking, of both the genre itself and the historical situation' – and 'in the nuclear sense of the *critical mass*' (Moylan, 1986: 10, emphases in original). To this double meaning of critical, I suggest we add the dimension of *self*-critique in order to better understand the subjective experiences of utopian practice in intentional communities. The dynamic of self-critique within Auroville has already been highlighted, corroborating intentional community scholar Lucy Sargisson's (2000: 29) observations that these communities do not claim to be perfect and that their members are 'often excessively critical of their community'. This is certainly true of Auroville, and I would argue that it is key to fuelling a continued process of perfectibility.

Of hope, Bloch (1986: 3) says: 'it is in love with success rather than failure'. Yet, Fredric Jameson (quoted in Sargisson, 2000: 122) points out that utopias 'have something to do with failure, and tell us more about our own limits and weaknesses than they do about perfect societies'. Sargisson (2000: 112) herself has remarked that they are 'a mirror to the present designed to bring out flaws', while Sargent (2010: 127) remarks that 'Utopia is … a life of hope. … We can hope, fail, and hope again. We can live with repeated failure and still improve the societies we build.'

In the Auroville context, the ideals of the community, as outlined in its founding texts (*A Dream*, *The Auroville Charter* and *To Be a True Aurovilian*

[The Mother, 1954, 1968, 1971]), articulate and inspire the collective hope of the community; yet, at the same time, they are a constant gauge against which Aurovilians critique themselves and each other. The spiritual world view of Integral Yoga plays a crucial role in framing, and assists in weathering, our 'disappointment' with the human limitations and flaws that we Aurovilians routinely face in ourselves and others in community life and development. According to this world view, such limitations are symptomatic of the overarching stage of the spiritual consciousness in which humanity is presently caught. Importantly, since it maintains that this spiritual consciousness is in a process of evolution and that we can choose to actively participate in it, this spiritual world view is also key to sustaining hope. As such, it is crucial for prevailing with the project of Auroville in the face of what Sargisson (2000: 2) observes are the 'frustrating' challenges of utopian practice.

To be faced by individual and collective limitations in the face of attempting to embody high ideals is no easy undertaking, and Sargent (2010: 49) rightly observes that intentional communities, due to their immersive nature, are a particularly intensive experience of this: 'ultimately utopianism is the transformation of everyday life. And intentional communities are particularly radical in that their members are willing to experiment with the transformation of their own lives. And all members of intentional communities must deal with this transformation every day.' While this challenging process provokes considerable self-criticism within intentional communities, Sargisson (2000: 29) also highlights that members 'see themselves as playing a transformative role' and view their communities as spaces in which change is possible and can at the very least be explored. Being empowered to actively and intentionally (re)shape lifestyles, practices and forms of social organization through ongoing experimentation thus keeps hope alive through enactment. In the Auroville context, this hope is embedded, legitimized and sustained for many within a broader vision and commitment to Integral Yoga's ontology of spiritual evolution.

It should be noted that the ways in which Aurovilians articulate the community's ideals are shared as well as contested, something that also contributes to internal frictions and frustrations, sometimes long-lived. While 'unity in diversity' (Sri Aurobindo, 1972: 499), a core principle in Sri Aurobindo's body of work, is one of Auroville's ideals of community, navigating difference is not always easy in practice, especially when it comes to realizing the community's lofty goals. An early statement by The Mother (2003b: 187) (displayed on the landing page of Auroville's website) states: 'Auroville wants to be a universal town where men and women of all countries are able to live in peace and progressive harmony above all creeds, all politics and all nationalities. The purpose of Auroville is to realise human unity.' As we have seen, the community is fractured at present over a forcefully implemented development agenda, which some feel is an opportunity to secure the manifestation of a 'city' as envisioned by Auroville's spiritual founder and others consider to be disrespectful of residents and their achievements, and detrimental to fostering their collaboration and participation moving forward, while such engagement was also envisioned as a path towards realizing a unique township. Similarly, there have been long-term, competing understandings of how to operate as an economy: some prioritizing income generation towards achieving a self-sufficient township; others envisioning a complete departure from the capitalist system.

In *The Symbolic Construction of Community*, Anthony Cohen (1989: 16) argued that while a repertoire of symbols held in common is what enables members to construct and maintain a sense of community, 'the sharing of the symbol is not necessarily the sharing of the meaning'. A community could contain a diversity of interpretations and relationships to communal symbols, so that it effectively 'incorporates and encloses difference' (Cohen, 1989: 74). This 'symbolic construction' (Cohen, 1989) of community is key to understanding the anarchic nature of Auroville's communal utopian practice – one in which community members with divergent views and approaches nonetheless espouse common ideals – which is completely distinct to that of blueprinted utopian communities, in which a uniformity of beliefs, attitudes and practices, achieved by the submission of individuals to the collective, is often assumed.

In the following chapters, I will focus on collective aspects of community life by exploring how community members have intentionally engaged with Auroville's ideals in the development of the community's institutions. I will continue to refer to the experiences of those that hold the official status of Aurovilian, though the term could be used to refer to a wider demographic, including the community's employees or volunteers, for example. I restrict myself to Aurovilians because only they can participate in the community's decision-making processes and administrative groups, or manage its enterprises and services. However, an exploration of whether and how the community's ideals shape the engagement of non-Aurovilian individuals active within the township (yet to be undertaken) could yield significant insights, for example, for the social reproduction of utopian practice.

As evidenced by the more personal nature of pursuits highlighted in this chapter, embodying consciousness is essential in defining these as spiritually prefigurative – a process echoed in the collective context of Auroville's participatory decision-making processes (explored in Chapter 5). It is also central to the understanding of what it means to become Aurovilian. I say 'become' because 'Aurovilian' is perceived not simply as the formal status of 'community member' but as an ideal: that of a 'willing servitor of the Divine Consciousness' (The Mother, 1968), which many consider themselves to be only working towards and that can thus itself be considered spiritually prefigurative in nature: 'A servitor of the divine consciousness is something I am not always ready for, to say the least. ... But I know that the main seed, the main drive is there, it is deeply rooted. ... I feel it is the idea of my life on earth' (Respondent #47, quoted in Clarence-Smith and Tewari, 2016: 18).

PART II

Polis

4

Divine Anarchy? The Development of the Auroville Polity

Introduction

'What political organisation do you want for Auroville?', someone asked The Mother in 1972, four years after the founding of the community. 'An amusing definition occurs to me', she replied: 'a divine anarchy' (The Mother, 2003b: 218). When she passed away in 1973, just five years after Auroville was founded, she left no blueprint for Auroville, no plan for how it should be governed – in her words, 'organised' (The Mother, 1977: 70) – nor any designated individuals who should assume this responsibility. While utopian communities were historically based on ideal blueprints that predetermined how society should be organized, Auroville was to be a prefigurative polity, destined to develop in tandem with the progressive spiritualization of its members. The kind of society that would emerge from this could not be anticipated: 'Men must become conscious of their psychic being and organise themselves spontaneously, without fixed rules and laws – that is the ideal' (The Mother, 2003b: 218).

In this chapter, we will explore the nature and development of Auroville as a polity, a community that has succeeded in sustaining and developing itself over 50 years, while securing autonomous arrangements for its internal administration. Even with this experiment in self-governance being presently threatened by the intervention of government-appointed administrators,[1] its unique trajectory provides an unparalleled opportunity to assess the viability and evolution of horizontal modes of prefigurative collective decision-making and organization. While modes of horizontal organizing are used across various alternative political contexts, including social movements like Occupy Wall Street that are significantly larger in terms of participants than intentional communities, the scope of enactment of intentional communities is broader than that of organizing protests given that they seek to establish alternative societies. Auroville is an exceptionally large and long-lasting community to have engaged in a horizontal exercise of governance, and studying its experience in doing so yields rich insights into issues raised by participants and researchers regarding the sustainability, effectiveness and equitability of such forms of radical political practice (Graeber, 2013; Rowe and Carroll, 2015; Hardt and Negri, 2017).

Examining Auroville's unique relationship with the Indian government will offer nuanced points of consideration for how alternative societies might navigate the challenges of embeddedness in a mainstream political context and engage with mainstream institutions of power. At present, a clear premise of contemporary prefiguration scholars and activists who focus on alternative forms of organizing and decision making in social movements is that such prefigurative politics articulate an alternative to the state and that to ally with, or make demands of, the government perforce invalidates their prefigurative nature (Graeber, 2013; van de Sande, 2015). Although controversial in this regard, Auroville's formal affiliation with the Indian state presents a critical dimension for proponents of prefigurative movements to examine given that among the key criticisms of prefigurative politics is that these fail to produce lasting social change precisely due to a lack of engagement with existing institutions (Mouffe, 2013: 111). For many years, this relationship provided an interesting case study of how an alternative society could be embedded in a facilitative superseding institutional framework (Clarence-Smith and Monticelli, 2022), though the recent interference of government authorities in the governance of the community shows the precariousness of this position.

We will investigate these critical questions and issues related to prefiguring political alternatives as we analyse Auroville's historical trajectory as a collective entity, from a founding period marked by the charismatic authority of The Mother to a struggle for self-determination supported by the Indian government and its courts, the concurrent establishment of its internal modes and practices of organization, and their evolution. The significance of the recent challenge to the community's self-governance will also be evoked but cannot be exhaustively examined given that it is ongoing at the time of writing.

Guru guidance and consensus culture: Auroville's early years and beyond

Let us begin by understanding the involvement of The Mother, as the spiritual founder of Auroville, in the first years of the community while she was still alive (1968–73). The Mother never lived in Auroville, insisting that it should be self-organized. She nonetheless acted as a de facto guru, or charismatic leader. Founding community members frequently sought her guidance on various matters – both large and small, as well as communal and personal – and by their accounts, her authority was uncontested (Auroville Radio, 2017b). To this day, her charismatic authority remains at play, arguably 'routinized' (Leard, 1993): statements she made about how Auroville should be managed and organized (see The Mother, 1977, 2003b; Guigan, 2018) are deployed by members to lend weight to their proposals and decisions (or their criticisms of those of others).

The Mother did envision what Auroville's (political) organization might be: ultimately, 'an organisation which is the expression of a higher consciousness working to manifest the truth of the future' (The Mother, 2003b: 198). That said, she also anticipated that a makeshift, temporary solution would have to be exercised while the polity matured spiritually towards embodying this. At one point, she suggested a 'hierarchical organisation grouped around the most enlightened centre' (The Mother, 1977: 70), similar to the concept of 'philosopher kings' that Plato proposed in *The Republic* (Plato and Adam, 1963). However, the radical political culture that had emerged in the 1960s and 1970s forefronted the feminist and anarchist non-hierarchical, collectivist practices of decision making based on consensus, and like many other intentional communities of this era, this was the form and ethos that was adopted in Auroville – from its early years, including while The Mother was alive.

This ethos remains strong today, even as the community has moved towards more representative models of governance internally (and has recently been subject to the pressures of hierarchical external authority from government officials). Such a transition is part of a broader phenomenon of formalization, institutionalization and bureaucratization in the Auroville context – one that Weber predicts for any form of organization or association as it scales and persists over time, especially after the death of a charismatic leader (Weber et al, 1978). That said, new policies and processes are constantly being internally challenged and revised,[2] a dynamic congruent with something The Mother had insisted on: that there should be nothing fixed, no rules in Auroville, in order to leave space for constant evolution (see The Mother, 2003a: 261, 266).

While it is the development and experience of the community's internal, experimental political practices, processes and forms of organization that are central to this book, the broader context in which Auroville is embedded is key to understanding how this 'real utopia' (Wright, 2010) has been enabled, as well as challenged. Auroville does not exist in a vacuum, and there has always been a legal body that has served to define the project before the government of India and exercise a degree of control over it. Before delving further into its internal development as a polity, we should seek to understand the frame in which this was exercised.

Divine intervention? Auroville's trajectory as a legal entity

When The Mother established Auroville in 1968, she registered the project under the Sri Aurobindo Society, a not-for-profit organization and research institute that she had founded in 1960. Following her death in 1973, the Sri Aurobindo Society sought to inherit the authority she had exercised over the community and withheld funds donated to Auroville as part of a bid for power in overseeing its management and development. This led to a court case that resulted, in the first instance, in the passing of the Auroville Emergency Provisions Act 1980 by the government of India. As per the act, the management of all Auroville assets were temporarily vested in the central government, stripping the Sri Aurobindo Society from any power over the community. In 1988, Auroville's status was finalized with the passing of the Auroville Foundation Act 1988, which established Auroville as a foundation, a statutory body under the auspices of the Ministry of Education of India's central government (see Minor,1999; Bernard, 2010; Auroville, 2015).

The chief architect of the act, Dr Kireet Joshi, was a devotee of The Mother and Sri Aurobindo – a civil servant who had joined the Sri Aurobindo Ashram in 1956 and had later been requested by The Mother to rejoin the Indian government, thereafter acting as her 'instrument'. His position enabled him to secure the first recurring source of funding from the Ministry of Education for Auroville via the establishment of an educational research institution in the community, the SAIIER, and later to propose the structure of the Auroville Foundation.

Having been close to The Mother, Dr Joshi had an in-depth understanding of her vision for Auroville and a commitment to serve its manifestation. Having been a civil servant, he was also well aware of the challenges and opportunities inherent in its incorporation into the Indian government. He was the perfect person to design a legal entity that would best safeguard and facilitate the development of Auroville, while fitting into the framework of the Indian government. That said, Dr Joshi did not try to fit Auroville into existing moulds but designed the Auroville Foundation Act to be something unique and outside the box – especially in that it incorporated an international overseeing body and gave Auroville residents jurisdiction and decision-making powers over Auroville's internal affairs.

The fact that such a tailored-to-Auroville act was passed – unanimously in both Houses of Parliament – is seen by many contemporary Aurovilians as having been facilitated by a higher spiritual power and strongly contributes to a discourse of the community being an exceptional and unique project that is spiritually chaperoned and protected (Auroville Radio, 2017b). The Indian government's endorsement of the project of a spiritual township aligns with a larger discourse that celebrates India as a uniquely spiritually inclined nation, a notion upheld by its founders (as well as other Indian spiritual leaders, such as Swami Vivekananda and Parmahansa Yogananda), who affirmed that the role of the Indian nation in the global context is to transmit its spiritual knowledge to serve humanity as a whole:

> India is the guru of the nations, the physician of the human soul in its profounder maladies; she is destined once more to new-mould the life of the world and restore the peace of the human spirit. (Sri Aurobindo, 1908)

> From the spiritual standpoint, India is the leading country in the world. Her mission is to give the example of spirituality. (The Mother, 1998: 232)

But how has the Auroville project been perceived and supported by the Indian government over time? Several Indian political leaders have paid dignitary visits to the community, each making positive statements on Auroville (Auroville, 2020a). The first was Prime Minister Indira Gandhi in 1969 (see Figure 4.1), who was later instrumental in the passing of the

Figure 4.1: Indian Prime Minister Indira Gandhi's first dignitary visit to Auroville, 6 October 1969

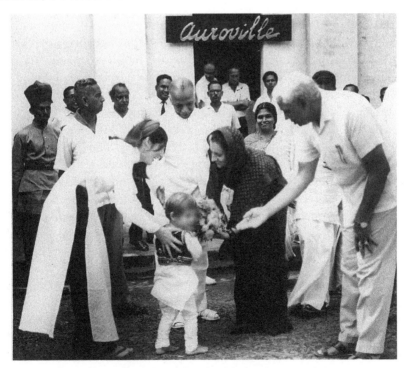

Source: Anonymous photographer (Auroville Digital Archives).

Auroville Emergency Provisions Act 1980. Prime Minister Rajiv Gandhi granted Aurovilians an audience during the lead-up to the Auroville Foundation Act 1988, which he ensured would be favourable to Auroville (Bernard, 2010).

These were leaders of India's Congress Party, who held power from India's independence until 2014, that is, at the time of Auroville's founding and for most of Auroville's existence. One of the main aims of the Congress Party was to uphold India as a secular nation state. This governmental stance has changed since 2014, when the BJP defeated the Congress Party and became the main ruling party. The BJP is a Hindu nationalist party that has been in power ever since.

While India has a majority of Hindus, whose religion is based on Vedic scripture, it is important to note that the country has other long-standing indigenous spiritual and religious traditions, such as Buddhism, Sikhism and Jainism. These are currently excluded from the national representation of Indian spirituality, as is the spirituality practised by India's tribal (Adivasi) groups, let alone non-indigenous religions practised by religious minorities in India: Christians, Muslims, Jews and Parsis (see Varshney, 2014). Although India's Vedic, yogic tradition has long been the face of Indian spirituality before the rest of the world, the BJP government has actively marketed it, creating the 'International Yoga Day' holiday and introducing a 'Yoga visa' for visitors to India.

In February 2018, Narendra Modi, the country's first BJP prime minister, visited the community to mark its 50th anniversary. Following a meditation in the Matrimandir, Auroville's spiritual centre, he gave a speech exhorting the community's ideals and activities over the past five decades, linking these to India's Vedic spiritual tradition (Modi, 2018). Narendra Modi is famous for his spiritual activities – photos of him meditating in a secluded cave in the Himalayas to seek spiritual communion at the eve of his re-election in May 2019 made headlines and Twitter feeds (Elsa, 2019). The BJP government has been newly and actively promoting Sri Aurobindo as a spiritual and a nationalist figure, and have also sought to accelerate Auroville's development, driven by the occasion of Aurobindo's 150th birth anniversary on 15 August 2022, which coincides with the anniversary of India's independence. This has caused many in the community and beyond to express concerns that after many years of relative autonomy, Auroville is now being co-opted for a larger political agenda.

Beyond the Indian context, Auroville has also long been recognized and endorsed by UNESCO (featuring in five UNESCO resolutions to date) given the community's alignment with UNESCO's core values, notably, of peace and harmony, cultural diversity, lifelong education, and sustainability (Auroville, 2022b). The combination of both national and international recognition with an incorporated status under an Indian government ministry that grants Auroville legal status and protection is significant, especially in light of the history of intentional communities. Most of these communal experiments have dissolved in the face of pressure and prejudice from the surrounding, dominant host society and its government institutions, often precipitated by the fact that their alternative practices did not fit into existing legal frameworks.[3] The Auroville community has recently experienced an unprecedented abuse of power by a government-appointed administration seeking to impose a development agenda, from the takeover of key community services like its media office to residents being threatened with eviction from their homes and workplaces, and even deportation (in the case of foreign individuals), when they are seen to contest the actions of this administration (see Stand for Auroville Unity, no date). However, the community's legal standing, as defined by the Auroville Foundation Act 1988, is currently being used to defend its Residents' Assembly in India's courts; the outcomes of these cases are pending and will determine to what extent the act is able to secure the 'autonomous arrangements' envisioned for the project (in the Auroville Foundation Act 1988).

'Autonomous arrangements': the Auroville Foundation Act 1988

As defined in the Auroville Foundation Act 1988, the Auroville Foundation has three authorities: the International Advisory Council, the Governing Board and the Residents' Assembly – together responsible for the 'management and further development of Auroville in accordance with its original Charter' (Preamble of the Auroville Foundation Act 1988). The Residents' Assembly is composed of all adult members of the community and is responsible for all day-to-day management, administration and decision making. To carry out these responsibilities, it forms and selects a number of 'working groups' to take up various aspects of community life (see Chapter 5). The parliamentary debates that led to the passing of the Auroville Foundation Act 1988 evoke the importance of these 'autonomous arrangements' for the development of Auroville, 'so that activities of Auroville can grow under an atmosphere conducive to harmonious growth' (Auroville Foundation Act 1988). It should also be noted that there is no Indian police force or other form of Indian law enforcement service within Auroville; rather, the community has been free to develop its own conflict-resolution modalities and safety and security service, though the security team does interact with the local police, primarily to address offences perpetrated by non-Aurovilians within the Auroville area (Datla, 2014).

The Governing Board is composed of Indian citizens appointed by the central government (usually connected to the government and familiar with Sri Aurobindo's philosophy) and is vested with the 'general superintendence' of the Auroville Foundation (Section 11.3 of the Auroville Foundation Act

1988). The Governing Board typically meets in Auroville twice a year and is briefed on pertinent issues by its secretary, a government-appointed official stationed in Auroville, and by the Working Committee, a body constituted by the act, consisting of Aurovilians selected by the Auroville Residents' Assembly to represent the interests of community members before the other official bodies of the Auroville Foundation.

The Governing Board, in turn, is advised by the International Advisory Council, a body composed of eminent international figures,[4] also appointed by the central government (Auroville, 2021b). The incorporation of an international advisory council is in keeping with The Mother's conception of Auroville as an international township. Such indications were intentionally heeded in the design of the act, as reported in the parliamentary debates pertaining to its passing: 'It is Sri Aurobindo and The Mother who provide the vision for Auroville and the proposed Foundation is intended to provide the infrastructure' (Section 1 of the Auroville Foundation Act 1988).

The central government appoints a secretary of the Auroville Foundation to conduct the legal and financial administration of the latter, under the authority of the Governing Board. This includes such duties as endorsing visa applications for non-Indian Aurovilians, authorizing the creation of entities (trusts) within which Auroville's economic activities are accounted, filing Auroville's income tax returns and overseeing the purchase, sale and protection (from encroachment) of Auroville land. While the Auroville Foundation Secretariat at first undertook the management of Auroville's funds and assets, it has since been the responsibility of an Aurovilian working group, the Funds and Assets Management Committee (FAMC), formed on the request of the Governing Board in 2007. The secretary of the Auroville Foundation[5] and its financial officer are officially members of the FAMC, but active participation in the FAMC's meetings is at their discretion. During my fieldwork period, neither the secretary nor the financial officer attended FAMC meetings, requested its notes or otherwise involved themselves in its decision-making processes; a previous officer chose to attend regularly, while another declined to attend at all. Even those who choose not to attend its meetings retain the authority to influence the FAMC's scope of work and decisions, for example, by requesting the committee to take up an issue that comes to their attention or countering decisions the group has taken. Matters pertaining to legal financial administration are within the purview of these officers of the Auroville Foundation Office (AVFO) and require their specific approval (such as the creation of new trusts).

A recently appointed secretary has taken unprecedented steps to limit the sphere of action of the Residents' Assembly and its working groups, including the FAMC; Dr Ravi has constituted a new FAMC of her choosing, reconstituting it as a committee of the Governing Board, not of the Residents' Assembly. Such actions are being legally contested by members of the Residents' Assembly and its representative body (the Working Committee). Historically, the Governing Board has occasionally made requests of certain Auroville working groups or institutions to take up new initiatives or lines of management. My limited insight into this dynamic – based on observations of meetings of the Governing Board and its members – is that the latter are rarely brought to term by the Residents' Assembly because the suggestions of Governing Board members are made with little familiarity of the complexity and political will of the Auroville context, and because they require resources that the community does not have, most importantly, human resources. So far, this has not resulted in any major rift, and it is important to note that the line between the Governing Board's mandated 'general superintendence' and the Residents' Assembly's mandated management of day-to-day affairs has never been clearly drawn, though this may be an outcome of the aforementioned court cases given that the authority of the secretary of the Auroville Foundation is coupled with that of the Governing Board (for a visual representation of the institutional structure of the Auroville Foundation, see Figure 4.2).

Given recent events, it is especially pertinent to highlight that the Auroville Foundation Act has provided a *facilitative* legal framework for the realization of some of Auroville's key ideals. The tripartite body of the Auroville Foundation allows for the development of an Aurovilian society as decided upon, and enacted by, an entirely Aurovilian body politic – the Residents' Assembly – and this allows for freedom of experimentation, formulation and reformulation, as intended by The Mother in accordance with the emerging needs and spiritual progress of current residents. The Indian government also grants Aurovilians five-year entry visas, unique in India, which allow foreign members to reside and work within Auroville, and thus realize its aspiration of being an international township. Furthermore, the legal-economic structure of the Auroville Foundation is such that all of its funds and immovable assets are vested within it, effectively enabling the economic ideal of 'no private property' and of non-ownership of the project, as specified in *The Auroville Charter* (The Mother, 1968). This is significant to note because alternative economic practices – based on non-individual and non-capitalist forms – in intentional community contexts and beyond are among the many that struggle to be legalized; the legal status of cooperatives is a rare example of success in this regard (see Birchall, 1997).

In addition to legal restrictions, financial pressure has also historically compromised the viability of other intentional community projects (leading Oneida, for example, to restructure as a joint-stock company); thus, it is important to highlight that the Indian government makes a yearly grant to Auroville for its research and infrastructure. One of the grant's beneficiaries is the SAIIER, which funds much of Auroville's experimental educational institutions and projects. This directly facilitates Auroville realizing itself as

Figure 4.2: Institutional structure of the Auroville Foundation

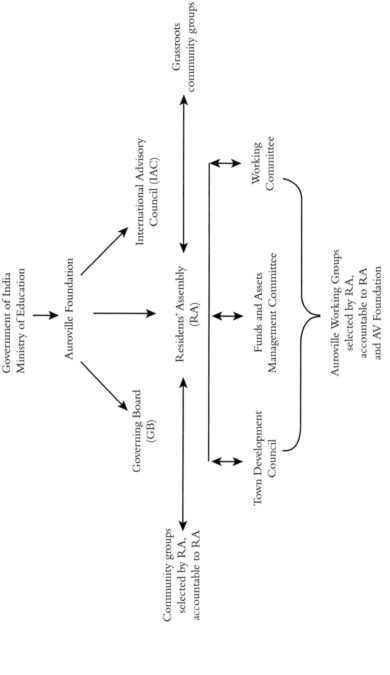

Source: Clarence Smith and Monticelli/Springer Nature (2022).

a site of unending education, one of the key points of its charter (Clarence-Smith, 2019b). L'Avenir d'Auroville (now known as the Auroville Town Development Council [ATDC]), Auroville's town-planning body, is another beneficiary, receiving annual funding for roads and infrastructure. Some of Auroville's working groups – the Working Committee, FAMC and ATDC – also receive funding for member stipends and basic expenditures (such as office expenses and member training). In addition to these recurring grants, community members have been successful in obtaining government funding for specific projects (all allocations of grants from the government of India are approved by the Governing Board). A recent example is the residential project Humanscapes, allocated to Auroville youth, the majority of whom do not have the financial resources to secure their own housing (Herbert, 2017).

The fact that Auroville receives significant funding from the government of India is celebrated by some community members and associates, and is a cause of concern for others. That this funding comes with its own restrictions favours the development of certain sectors or aspects of Aurovilian society, ones that may not be congruent with the community's own development priorities – a key example being the funding of buildings that exceed the needs of the current population, which is then compelled to bear the costs of their ongoing maintenance. While a recent push for urban development has come from the secretary and the Governing Board, building projects have historically been proposed by community members, not the Indian government. However, in recent decades, the community has not undergone a collective process to determine what its funding priorities should be and budget requests for grants from the government of India – or from other international funding bodies – did not therefore base themselves on a community mandate of development (though they were reviewed and approved by teams of Aurovilians appointed and overseen by the Working Committee and FAMC, who are, in turn, selected by the Residents Assembly or the Aurovilian executives of government-funded institutions within Auroville, such as the SAIIER and Bharat Nivas, Auroville's 'Pavilion of India').

It should be noted, however, that in early 2022, the community's Budget Coordination Committee (BCC) held a participatory budgeting process to identify priority funding areas for the township's municipal budget. While the scope of this budget – primarily financed by Auroville's own economic activities (BCC, 2022) – is limited to sustaining Auroville community members and public services, the FAMC hoped to scale this process to seek inputs on Auroville's overarching funding needs. A development priorities study has also been conducted in recent years (Ayer et al, 2021) and is slated for community consultation and eventual ratification. Meanwhile, (as mentioned in Chapter 3), a unique participatory planning process that seeks to inform Auroville's development with the visions, values and aspirations of the Auroville community has been piloted (Aggarwal et al, 2022).

Alter-development and the state: government-enabled anarchy?

As we have seen, Auroville's unique status within the legal framework of the Indian government sanctions that the community should retain autonomy over its internal affairs, enabling it to be self-managing and to experiment with alternative practices, while benefiting from government endorsement and funding. Considering that legal and financial pressure has compromised the viability of other intentional community projects, this may be one key to its longevity. However, scholars have expressed concerns around the potential co-optation of the project as a result of its relational enmeshment with the Indian government, as well as its embeddedness in a capitalist context (Horassius, 2013; Monticelli, 2018). Since the completion of those studies, residents have come face to face with this risk given the attempted imposition of a development agenda by government-appointed authorities of the Auroville Foundation (notably, the Governing Board and its secretary) and the latter's constitution of parallel committees to those of the Residents' Assembly (notably, the Working Committee, FAMC and ATDC) – matters that have been brought to India's courts since late 2021. While these developments invite us to rest with the argument that government and alternative projects are necessarily pitted against one another, recent research points to an alternative assessment – and Auroville's historical relationship with the Indian government does compel us to at least consider the role of the state in facilitating its development as a prefigurative alternative (Clarence-Smith and Monticelli, 2022).

The economist Mariana Mazzucatto (2013, 2018) highlights the little-known role that governments already play in enabling innovative development, as the critical funders of early-stage research into alternative practices that can eventually reshape entire industries towards the public good. This stands in contrast to the narrative that the private sector fuels innovation; furthermore, such investment is predicated on financial return, rather than social and environmental benefit – which is the primary objective of government (and non-governmental organization) grants to Auroville. Government grants to Auroville are thus, importantly, free of co-optation by the logic of the market and help to buffer the community from its pressures. While a primary source of external funding to Auroville, currently and historically, comes from the government of India and charitable foundations, not corporations, it is relevant to note that both national and international corporations have recently financed projects in Auroville as part of their corporate social responsibility schemes.[6]

As mentioned earlier, a key concern surrounding alternative organizations and practices is the risk of them being co-opted by the dominant capitalistic world order (Decreus et al, 2014; Smucker, 2014; Monticelli, 2018). Yet, prefiguration scholar Lara Monticelli questions the assumption that the types of alliances Auroville has with government and industry necessarily imply co-optation, and asks instead whether these might be an indicator of the success of a prefigurative project:

> Isn't it exactly when a municipality, a state, a supranational institution or even a multinational corporation starts to recognize ... a 'best practice' and ... to encourage its growth through funds and favourable policies, that prefigurative movements can consider themselves as having succeeded in their goal? Or is this co-optation nullifying their efforts? (Monticelli, 2018: 513)

Whether Auroville will be a victim of its own success, attracting more interest from the current government that it may wish for, resulting in an undermining of its experimental community processes and the alternatives these may prefigure, is an open question. Another is whether Auroville can be considered a prefigurative project despite its enmeshment with the government.

A central argument of prefigurative actors (and their sympathetic scholars) is that 'emancipation within, acceptance by, or incorporation into current power structures' (van de Sande, 2015: 178) nullifies the prefigurative nature of their political practice because the very premise of prefigurative practice is to elaborate alternatives – in the case of prefigurative politics, to dominant, formal political institutions. Some scholars, however, point out that the failure of prefigurative movements to achieve any substantial or sustainable political and social change (such as Occupy Wall Street) may be due to, and possible remedied by, engaging with the state and its institutions (Mouffe, 2013; Rowe and Carroll, 2015). Prefiguration scholar Davina Cooper (2020) invites us to consider the latter as 'necessary sites for transformative action' that 'should not be discounted when it comes to prefigurative practice'. She also charts the potential for a prefigurative state, one whose key features resemble those of Auroville's internal governance, which we turn to next (Cooper, 2017).

Thomas Moore's literary utopia, and many others, are conceived as islands, disconnected from the real world – and criticized for their irrelevance as a result, as were utopian community projects that tried to isolate themselves from the contexts in which they were, nonetheless, necessarily embedded. Today, it seems disingenuous to require prefiguratively utopian projects to be of the world but not to engage with it. There is no utopian formula that can ensure the degree of boundedness required for experimenting with alternatives and simultaneously sustain the enmeshment that seems critical to the sustainability and success of such projects. However, a dynamic, reflexive balance – and perhaps even a degree of compromise – between seclusion and engagement seems to be essential in the process of prefiguring, developing and embedding 'real utopias' (Wright, 2010).

How does the Auroville community govern itself?

Now that we have explored the legal and governmental context in which the Auroville community is embedded, let us turn to its 'autonomous arrangements'. What political organization has developed in the community, and how has it evolved over time? What propels this evolution, and how successful or satisfactory do its members consider it to be? What insights can this offer into the viability and desirability of alternative political models, particularly in a post-COVID-19 era in which strengthening local governance and organizing has emerged as essential, and in which national governments in democratic states are failing to foster unity, equitability and sustainability? Can we consider Auroville to be a 'prefigurative polity'?

As already mentioned, the community has a long history of collective decision-making processes, but it has also developed representative structures within its overarching horizontal political organization. In its early years, when made up of only a few hundred people, decision making was undertaken collectively at weekly community meetings, in which any Aurovilian could raise a topic and express their resonance or concern with the issues raised to arrive at a consensus (see Figure 4.3). As the community grew and became more complex, 'working groups' were formed to take responsibility for specific aspects through bottom-up processes initiated by community members and agreed upon collectively.

Figure 4.3: Auroville community meeting (Certitude), 1980

Source: Anonymous photographer (Auroville Digital Archives).

These 'working groups' – named as such to indicate that they were not to be committees of individuals disconnected from the actual work of the community – include ones mandated to oversee aspects of the community at large, such as funds and assets management (the FAMC) or town planning (the ATDC). While their members are selected by the community at large in a selection process of its design, there are also sector-level groups that include grass-roots collectives made up of anyone active within the sector (for example, all farmers are de facto members of the Farm Group, while all foresters are members of the Forest Group). Although these groups take responsibility for the administration of their respective sectors, they are overseen by a community-selected working group (in the case of the Farm Group and Forest Group, the FAMC).

In the past, several groups with overarching community mandates were composed of members of various sector groups of Auroville as representatives appointed by the latter (up to 2017, the FAMC was composed of representatives of the Farm Group and Forest Group, alongside those of other sectors, such as the Housing Group). Transitioning to 'participatory working groups', whose members were selected from and by the community at large, is arguably a shift towards more of a representative than a direct democratic model, though, interestingly, it was effectuated to further democratize and collectivize governance in Auroville by making it possible for any community member to occupy roles previously reserved for active stakeholders, as well as mandating the inclusion of a 'resource pool' of Aurovilians to support working group teams (Study Group on Organisation, 2016). The use of the term 'participatory' reflects this broader inclusivity.

While there are pros and cons to each model – 'selected' and 'stakeholder' – it is important to note that in neither case could members of working groups be seen as representatives to whom Aurovilians transferred their political power. As the Residents' Assembly constitutes, selects and mandates its groups, and its meetings are the ultimate decision-making forum of the community, this authority lies not with working groups but with the community at large. Working groups must regularly publish reports of their meetings, and any major decisions – such as a new policy – must be brought to the Residents' Assembly for approval and, in some cases, the Governing Board for ratification.

The question of ratification is based on whether the working group in question is formally recognized by the Auroville Foundation and therefore interfaces with its Governing Board,[7] or whether it exists purely within the 'civil society' space of Auroville – which means it answers only to the Residents' Assembly and can be dissolved or changed at any time. That said, the structure, membership, selection and functioning of even those working groups formally recognized by the Auroville Foundation are designed and can be amended by the Residents' Assembly. In fact, the very participatory working group model evoked earlier was ratified by the community to be adopted by Auroville for such working groups,[8] with an accompanying selection process (see Study Group on Organisation, 2016), in 2014 – and two of these have since undergone a community-led restructure.[9]

Importantly, working groups do not have the exclusive right to make a proposal to the community for ratification by the Residents' Assembly. The Residents' Assembly Service, the organization and communication platform at the service of the Residents' Assembly, calls these meetings on the request of either working groups or other residents. Often, it is proposals made by informal groups of concerned Aurovilians that drive change in the community, rather than the working groups officially in charge; the latter repeatedly report being bogged down in the firefighting of addressing pressing everyday issues in the area of community life they are responsible for.

This is a significant phenomenon to note, as it affirms the political potential and responsibilization of citizens who are empowered to shape their polities. Historically, civilian protest and social movements have driven change in many democratic societies – consider the women's liberation and civil rights movements. However, the demands these made nonetheless had to be accepted by politicians who had the exclusive right to write policy. In Auroville, anyone can design and propose a policy, or the amendment to a policy, and bring it to the community at large for ratification, without having to petition a working group to adopt it first. A recent example is the entry policy, which was amended in 2017 through such a process. As we will see in Chapter 7, community members have also instigated the provision of cooperative public services, thus performing an 'active citizenship' (Mori, 2014).

Working group members' terms vary in length from one to five years, and many pursue other roles in the community concurrently. My mother, for example, has been the executive of the Auroville Visitors Centre for almost 20 years and has also served on various working groups throughout this period. Only few Aurovilians are the equivalent to 'career' public servants, remaining exclusively engaged as working group members – a role that is not necessarily remunerated – shifting from one working group to another once their terms come to an end.

The turnover in working group membership, along with the magnitude of working groups in Auroville, has entailed that a significant number of Aurovilians have served in at least one of these at some point during their community membership. As a result, they have insight into the pertinent and often perennial issues of the community, and have undergone the exercise of engaging with these. This empowers them to continue to do so beyond their term as working group members by forming part of what I referred to earlier in this section as 'concern groups': associations of activist Aurovilians spearheading change in the community. Not infrequently, these politically active individuals are concurrently part of a working group.

Residents' Assembly decision-making processes

Despite this rich grass-roots political participation in Auroville, the number of people who attend Residents' Assembly meetings (RAMs) (see Figure 4.4) and vote in ensuing Residents' Assembly decisions (RADs) has historically been relatively small. Recent crisis topics have mobilized between ~700 and ~900 participants, though policy topics usually draw approximately ~200, which is less than 10 per cent of the adult Aurovilian population (Vidal, 2022).

While many Aurovilians and scholars of the community have used these figures as defining measures of 'low' political participation of Aurovilians,[10] it should be understood that many community members are engaged in forums at other scales more directly related to their areas of interest and activity and thus cannot be considered politically inactive. For instance, the monthly meetings of the Forest Group, which I sat in on during my fieldwork, were the best attended of any sector group I knew, but I only ever saw very few Forest Group members in Residents' Assembly meetings during that period.

In my observations and experience, virtually all aspects of community life and development in Auroville are constantly being deliberated and (re)defined at various scales and in various – and sometimes overlapping – collective processes. These are notoriously time-consuming and wearisome; even the staunchest proponents of such direct democratic practice concede that the engagement it requires is trying (Graeber, 2013). The sheer magnitude of such processes occurring in Auroville at any given time is overwhelming; even when dedicating myself full-time to doctoral field research, it was impossible to follow each, let alone be an active participant in them. When we consider this degree of routine political engagement that is embedded in everyday life in Auroville, and that this is at least part of the reason why people do not additionally participate in many community-wide processes, the attendance rates of the latter can no longer be considered an accurate indicator of the political activity of Aurovilians.

For example, the attendance of Forest Group members in Residents' Assembly meetings has sharply increased since 2021, when meetings related to the imposition of urban development agendas were being held, agendas that directly impact the work and vision of the Forest Group. While this could suggest a lack of interest in other community issues, it can also be understood as a way of limiting participation fatigue, an important concern in horizontal organizations of any scale (Hardt and Negri, 2017).

That said, it is important not to ignore dissatisfaction with the collective decision-making processes of the Residents' Assembly – much of which is common to direct and participatory democratic models and experiences worldwide – as a significant deterrent to participation. Specific points of dissatisfaction include the high investment in time, lack of confidence in an

Figure 4.4: General meeting at the Unity Pavilion, Auroville

Source: Marco Saroldi (Auroville Digital Archives).

actionable outcome, unpleasant interpersonal dynamics and the challenge of public speaking. The latter is compounded in Auroville's multinational context given that meetings are held in English, which makes them difficult not only to contribute to but also to even comprehend for the community's many non native English speakers. Furthermore, the sense of entitlement to speak is influenced by many factors, such as longevity in the community, education and gender, which inextricably and invisibly shape power dynamics even in horizontally designed assemblies.

Other consensus decision-making forums – notably, the Global Justice Movement and Occupy Wall Street – have tried to address some of these challenges with specific facilitation measures and practices to prefigure inclusive, equitable and efficient political forums, with varying levels of success (Graeber, 2013; Hardt and Negri, 2017). Recent attempts in Auroville include experimenting with a citizens' assembly model, in which community members are selected at random to be educated on various perspectives (often from experts) on a particular issue. Thus informed, they deliberate on and deliver a proposed way forward. The Auroville Citizens' Assembly Exploration Team saw potential in the model, increasingly used worldwide, for addressing key concerns related to the existing 'general assembly' model used in Residents' Assembly meetings: random selection would create an opportunity to reach out to Aurovilians who may not typically attend Residents' Assembly meetings and avoid having the same voices dominate such forums; offering participants education on the issue would respond to the concerns of those who do not feel informed enough to attend meetings or contribute to community decisions; and deliberating in small groups would ensure more people have the express opportunity to share their views, as well as listen to those of others (the model also includes skill building in recognizing bias and deep listening). While the Auroville Citizens' Assembly Exploration Team saw potential for prefiguring Auroville's founding ideals of unending education and human unity through this model (Aggarwal et al, 2021), a key concern in Auroville's decision-making processes in general is that the latter do not reflect the spiritualization that the community aspires to. Attempts to foster the latter have been experimented with, such as in the selection process of Auroville's working groups, which will be examined in depth in Chapter 5.

While both the citizens' assembly model and selection process use consensus-based forms of decision making, proposals brought to the community at large for a Residents' Assembly decision are currently ratified using a voting process. A Residents' Assembly decision requires that a proposal be presented at a community-wide meeting, in which counter-proposals are also invited. Following this presentation, feedback is invited on the proposal(s). This feedback is collected and shared by the Residents' Assembly Service with those bringing forward the proposal to assess and potentially incorporate. The revised proposal is then presented once again to the community in a Residents' Assembly meeting, and those present decide whether another round of feedback is required or whether they consider it ready to be brought to the community as a whole to decide on via a voting process held by the Residents' Assembly Service.[11] At present, a positive outcome is determined by a simple majority, while in the past, other conditions were in place: a quorum of participation in the voting process had to be met (10 per cent), and a high majority had to have voted 'yes' (at least 80 per cent). Voting, however, is a relatively recently formalized practice in Auroville; previously, decisions were typically taken by consensus at meetings of the Residents' Assembly. In general, it is a practice that is eschewed by groups practising consensus decision making because it neither allows for dialogue nor ensures outcomes that the vast majority of participants will be satisfied with, though in case of an impasse, a high majority vote is a common tool (Graeber, 2013).

While the recent Residents' Assembly decision-making process described earlier newly incorporates a structured feedback process, and the readiness of a proposal to be brought to a vote is a prerogative of community members, the practice of voting is not widely accepted in Auroville. Some consider voting to be poor decision-making practice because people who have not been part of a decision-making process on a particular issue can still vote on it, without having heard the proposal presented, questions asked, feedback offered and potential counter-proposals made – as such, they may be susceptible to lobbying or making uninformed decisions. Others find it to be a simple and obvious way to ensure participation of a wider group of community members than those who are able or inclined to attend Residents' Assembly meetings; indeed, a key criticism of consensus-based decision-making processes is that they are necessarily restricted to those who can commit the time required to do so and this disadvantages parents, caregivers and others with long working hours (Graeber, 2013).

Those who oppose voting include people who uphold that Auroville is a collective experiment and that we should aspire to arrive at a collective will, which is something distinct from a majority of individual wills or from achieving agreements between personal opinions, views and desires, which Aurovilians see as belonging to the realm of the individual ego. At a fundamental level, this idea of a collective will is related to the ideal of Auroville as a polity dedicated to prefiguring the 'Divine Will':

> At one time it was said that the Residents' Assembly's fundamental function is to arrive at an agreement. This statement is good, but not sufficient. It is not an instrument of agreement and disagreement. The starting-point is wrong. It is to mature, constantly, the sense of all of us as a collectivity, devoted to the Divine's will. (Clouston, 2003)

While a collective, spiritual maturation is clearly the project of Auroville as envisioned by The Mother, there have been proposals to shift from collective decision-making processes to hierarchical structures. A recent presentation made by a group of Aurovilians in 2022 ("Auroville Prosperity") included the proposal to experiment with a 'Unity Council'[12] composed of long-standing members of the community, based on the suggestion that The Mother (1977: 70) had made of a 'hierarchical organisation grouped around the most enlightened centre', while a collective spiritual maturation is in process towards an eventual 'divine anarchy'. While our extensive use of democratic processes overall is felt by many to be a poor exercise in prefiguring the spiritualized society aspired to, many still see collective decision-making processes as a fertile space for collective experimentation and potential maturation.

Is Auroville (in) a prefigurative state?

In her article 'Prefiguring the state', prefiguration scholar Davina Cooper (2017: 339) explores the potential for a prefigurative conceptualization and articulation of the state that 'rejects a sharp distinction between states and other political governance formations' and 'reimagines what statehood could mean'. She proposes that we broaden the category of statehood to 'differently scaled, bounded forms of institutionalised diversity', for instance, by recognizing 'micro, guerrilla and regional states' (Cooper, 2017: 350). While Cooper's article is theoretical, it offers an uncanny lens through which to understand the prefigurative nature of Auroville as a 'micro' state with an atypical boundedness given its insertion within a traditional nation state. For Cooper (2017: 343), a key determinant of a prefigurative polity is the involvement of its members in a 'constantly evolving governmental form'. Embeddedness in everyday relations is also central; she envisages that policies be 'advanced, transformed, gutted, enabled and thwarted' through 'a multiplicity of informal junctures and networks', and imagines overlapping and entangled roles of administrators and beneficiaries (Cooper, 2017: 343–5). Auroville's mode of self-governance is evident in these descriptions, and significantly, this embedded, prefigurative nature remains unchallenged by a seeming shift towards representative democracy.

It is important here to revisit critiques related to the sustainability and therefore political relevance of horizontal modes of prefigurative organizing in terms of proposing a viable alternative to the state. Some scholars consider that it is the very resistance to the incorporation of representative structures within prefigurative organizing that restricts its practice to 'temporary assemblies and smaller grassroots organizations' (Rowe and Carroll, 2015: 157). In light of the documented limitations of horizontal organizing – in terms of scale, efficiency, equitability and sustainability (see

Hardt and Negri, 2017) – even its supporters, such as political commentator Naomi Klein, have suggested that the principles of horizontalism are to be made 'compatible with the hard work of building structures and institutions' (Rowe and Carroll, 2015: 155).

It is precisely this compatibilization that the Auroville community has been engaged in, both internally, in its adoption of representative structures within a horizontal political organization, and externally, in its relationship with the Indian government, which has enshrined and – at least up until recently – left a significant degree of autonomy to this alternative organization. While some scholars maintain that prefigurative experiments will inevitably be disenfranchised in their engagements with mainstream political power, the Auroville community has had a more than 50-year history in which it has been able to continue to experiment with the development of its political organization and processes, despite the establishment of Auroville as a foundation (in 1988) entraining a formalization of certain of its representative bodies, or working groups. The Auroville Foundation Act recognizes the Residents' Assembly – all adult members of the Auroville community – as sovereign in determining the internal organization of the township. While there have been no major changes in the Residents' Assembly's mode of internal organization – such as empowering a spiritually enlightened elite to manage community affairs, a possibility that has been evoked – formally recognized working groups have undergone community-led restructuring, notably, both the ATDC and the FAMC in 2017.

Auroville's process of institutionalization is therefore flexible, enabling a responsiveness to the needs and wishes of the community. Such 'flexible institutionalisation' (Clarence-Smith and Monticelli, 2022) is key to embodying an arguably prefigurative state in Auroville; it may even provide an example for other alternatives negotiating relationships with mainstream political entities. That being said, Aurovilians themselves remain perennially dissatisfied with the state of their political practice and organization, both practically speaking, in terms of efficiency and inclusion, and in its ability to be prefigurative of Auroville's spiritual ideals. While horizontal organizing is currently considered the epitome of radical political practice, the community's long-standing (and virtually unparalleled[13]) enactment of the mode ought to compel those engaged in upholding it to imagine what may lie beyond.

For Aurovilians, this is strongly tied to a spiritually prefigurative practice, one that seeks to embody spiritually evolved individual and collective states, and in Chapter 5, we will explore how this was attempted in the context of a collective decision-making process in Auroville. In subsequent chapters, we will turn to examples of Auroville's alternative economic institutions and organizations, and explore how these sought to engage the community's ideals. The establishment and alternative workings of such bodies are another important aspect of Auroville's prefigurative institutionalization, contributing to the community's ability to move beyond the ephemeral performativity that prefigurative movements are criticized for to one that ensures social reproduction. Yet, concerns about co-optation raise a question as to whether Auroville will continue to exists as a unique case study in which to assess the viability and observe the trajectory of such hybrid forms of prefigurative organizing.

Spiritually Prefigurative Politics in Practice: An Embodied Account of an Auroville Community Decision-Making Process

Introduction

> One feels at times, that a decision could be reached more
> effectively by simply … quieting oneself, and in the most
> profound sense of the word, merge in Silence.
>
> Roy, 2014

It is a Thursday evening and a group of Aurovilians are gathered in the Awareness Through the Body Hall for our weekly sensory awareness session. For the first time, our facilitator has chosen to work with the 12 qualities identified by The Mother as essential to embody for an individual and collective spiritual evolution. She begins by reading out the names of each of the qualities and the description The Mother has given about them from a set of cards. As she does so, I find that one of them particularly resonates with me: Generosity. She then places each of the cards, face down on the floor and asks us to pick one: "If one card calls you, then pick that one, and if none of them calls you, then just pick at random", she says. We each pick the card, look at the quality and then place it back. Mine is Generosity.

We then proceed to individually explore embodying each of these qualities through various spontaneous physical forms, our facilitator verbally prompting and guiding us to express outwardly, with our bodies, the quality as we are experiencing it within us (see Figure 5.1). Once we have explored all 12, she guides us to create a collective shape, each embodying the quality they had originally picked. One by one, we add our bodies and our qualities to complement the growing form. I was very touched watching each person move and place themselves consciously, with depth of presence, care and

Figure 5.1: Awareness Through the Body intensive, Auroville

Source: Awareness Through the Body.

sincerity, their faces soft and receptive. I still remember the first one of my peers: her intentional and deliberate walk to the centre of the room, where she placed herself in a kneeling position, arms extended, embodying Sincerity. Once we had each joined the form, our facilitator guided us to feel the collective shape, and each of the qualities that we were embodying within it, repeating each of their names.

Like in so many Awareness Through the Body sessions, I was struck by the depth of interpersonal connection and collective presence that we were able to embody and cultivate with one another in this consciously facilitated space. After the session, I expressed that I often asked myself how we might be able to translate this experience into everyday lives – embody this state when working with one another, for instance. A fellow participant said that she had envisioned adopting some Awareness Through the Body practices in our political forums, certain it would have a positive effect on the latter.

Connecting spiritual and political practices is something that I have had many conversations about with others in Auroville. While we will be exploring the use of spirituality-informed practices in the collective decision-making processes of an explicitly spiritual intentional community, it is important to note that spiritual self-development practices are being increasingly adopted in a broad spectrum of political contexts. These range from prefigurative social movements like Occupy Wall Street (Writers for the 99%, 2012) to the US Congress (Seitz-Wald, 2013), while indigenous spiritual protocols have been central to protests that seek to protect sacred indigenous land, such as the currently ongoing Protect Mauna Kea demonstration in Hawai'i (Protect Mauna Kea, no date).

That said, spirituality is critiqued for rendering individuals apolitical, for two main reasons. The first is that it emphasizes a detachment from worldly life. The second is that in responsibilizing individuals for their experiences of hardship – whether economic, social or psychological – it draws emphasis away from seeking out and addressing the roots of such hardship in structural inequities and social reform, framing these instead as inadequate self-management (Rimke, 2000; Žižek, 2001; Davies, 2015; Madsen, 2015; Spicer, 2011; Saari and Harni, 2016).

It is important to note that this critique is based on Buddhist-based contemplative practices, such as mindfulness – though it does extend to a broader set of practices of secularized 'Eastern' mysticism, such as yoga – and that other academics have offered a counterpoint to this discourse. They highlight the instrumental influence of such contemplative spiritual practices in political engagement, arguing that these can not only trigger a more conscious participation but also 'assist in fighting burnout, political cynicism, and hopelessness' (Wilson, 2014: 185). As we shall see in this chapter, in the Auroville context, members' spiritual commitment to the project has sustained many through challenging collective processes.

In her work, political scientist and somatic facilitator Anita Chari (2016) differentiates between 'contemplative' (such as seated mindfulness meditation) and 'embodied' spiritual practices (such as tai chi or hatha yoga). She highlights the importance of the latter for developing relational capacities, which she argues may give rise to 'new political potentials' (Chari, 2016: 236), echoing the conversations I had in Auroville. Karen Litfin (2018) has also highlighted how the experience of individual and shared conscious states can act as an embodied reference to strive for in collective contexts, including political and decisional forums.

Having personally experienced it as a member of the Auroville community, I know that if people have had the experience of individual and shared conscious states, this will act as an embodied reference to strive for in collective contexts, including political and decisional forums – an extrapolation other scholars have made (Litfin, 2018). I have intentionally drawn from my experiences of shared conscious collective relational states in Awareness Through the Body sessions in participating in community decision-making forums. For example, I have used Awareness Through the Body techniques of withdrawing my attention from identification with emotional reactions or mental fixations on a particular issue, and actively centring it within myself, so that I could access a more grounded, harmonious, receptive and expanded state of presence and awareness. This enabled me to reconnect to the objectives of the process at hand, as well as to the others in the room.

Both Anita Chari (2016) and James Rowe (2015, 2016) specifically highlight the inclusion of both contemplative and embodied spiritual practices, such as meditation and yoga, in left-wing social movements like Occupy Wall Street. Rowe (2015) notes that 'Embodied practices such as singing and dancing, along with spiritual forms such as prayer and ceremony, have been central to most successful social movements' – even though such practices, regrettably, do not figure in the prefigurative literature on these movements:

> Practices like yoga and meditation were woven throughout Occupy, and were integral to its endurance and impact; they were not a sideshow. This is part of the Occupy story that remains untold, and yet holds vital lessons for the growing body of activists and mind/body practitioners wondering what good mindfulness can do in an unjust world. (Rowe, 2015)

In light of this, and the fact that the literature on prefiguration is largely focused on alternative organizational and decision-making practices, the current chapter is centred on the spiritualization of decision-making forums and practices in the Auroville context. Through an examination of the selection process for Auroville's participatory working groups, I explore the articulation between spirituality and political practice, furthering the debates outlined earlier on whether the former is instrumental and strategic for the latter, galvanizing and sustaining of conscious political participation.

The 'selection process': an embodied account of collective decision making in Auroville

Two selection processes for Auroville's participatory working groups held in 2017[1] will serve here as the basis for an ethnographic analysis of spiritually prefigurative politics. The first is that of the newly mandated ATDC 'Interface' team; the second is one in which new members of the Working Committee, FAMC and Auroville Council were selected. We will begin by exploring the use of spiritual prompts and practices throughout the selection process, assessing how these articulated with and informed its political aims. Next, we will focus on how spirituality shaped the participation of individuals in the process.

I attended both selection processes as a participant member of the community. At the time, any Aurovilian could nominate themselves or others to take part in the selection process, either as 'candidates' (those who are willing to take up a working group post) or 'participants' (people who want to participate in selecting members of the new working groups). Those nominated by others were free to accept or decline to participate, but to be selected to a working group, one had to attend the three-day selection process in its entirety. All who attended formed part of the Selection Committee, and 'participants' were eligible for selection as well as 'candidates': any participant could decide, up until the final day of the selection process, to put themselves forward as a candidate, and any candidate could choose to withdraw and continue as a participant at any point in the process. The statuses serve to indicate the attendees' initial, and potentially evolving, intentions with regard to their participation in the selection process.

Common reasons for declining a nomination were that people were too busy with other work in the community to consider joining a working group or were critical of the structure and practice of governance in Auroville and could not envisage themselves working within it. Others protested the selection process, which they considered to be too time-consuming, laborious and frustrating (it has been reviewed and modified almost annually since I participated in 2017). Those who decided to join as participants, beyond wanting to ensure that good teams were selected, were interested in participating in a collective process. Some specifically wished to support the selection process spiritually, most commonly through the practice of 'silent presence keeping' (elaborated on in the next section of this chapter).

I went to both selection processes with my mother, who runs the Auroville Visitors Center and had also been nominated for working groups. She had previously served on the ATDC and, although she was not considering doing so again, felt a certain responsibility to participate in the selection process for the new team given her experience. She was considering serving on the FAMC, having previously served in economic administration as the Auroville Board of Services representative to the BCC and being strongly committed to realizing Auroville's economic ideals. My father, who had served on working groups in the past and had been nominated as a candidate in the second selection process, declined to participate given the lengthiness and laboriousness of the process; in any case, he was not interested in joining a working group.

At the second selection process, less than 5 per cent of the adult population participated, something that proved to be a significant concern for many in the room, both because the choice of candidates would be small and because their selection would only be undertaken by a minority of the community at large. Since many ongoing and outgoing members of working groups attended the selection process given their investment in governance, the ratio of working group to non-working group participants was high, which further exacerbated the sentiment that a clique of people influence governance in Auroville.

I counted five people under the age of 35, including myself. When I asked peers who had been nominated why they had chosen not to attend, they echoed the concerns raised earlier: the process was too time-consuming; and they could not imagine themselves working within the current administrative culture due to its excessive emphasis on deliberation, rather than practical engagement. When I asked others why they had not signed up to be a 'participant' in the process, almost all were oblivious to the fact that it was even taking place or that one could participate without being a candidate, which pointed to an overall disengagement with Auroville's political administration at that time, a dynamic that has since shifted considerably.

Nonetheless, both of the selection processes drew Aurovilians active in different fields within the community, such as farming, forestry, dentistry, architecture, therapy, schooling, conflict resolution, commercial and social enterprise, community services (such as the Housing Service), and the Matrimandir. These included Jeroen, a Dutch man in his 40s, living in Auroville since 2003 with his wife and two children, who had worked with Auroville's farms for a decade and then set up a social entrepreneurship incubation platform for Tamil Nadu in affiliation with a nationwide organization. Another was Padma, a young woman in her early 30s, born and raised in Auroville to French and German parents. Padma was a former classmate of mine, who had gone on to obtain a master's in communications for business in France. Recently returned to Auroville, she currently served as secretary for one of the community's working groups, was a founding team member of a natural horsemanship centre and sang with me in the Auroville Choir. Renana, an Indian woman in her 60s, worked in Auroville's animal shelter and was a dedicated Aikido practitioner. She had joined Auroville in 1980 and had first been active in forestry. Arun, a local Tamil in his 40s, had grown up in Auroville, where he had been a schoolteacher – in a wide range of subjects, from Tamil language to theatre – for the past 15 years. Hector, a Catalan man, joined Auroville with his wife in 1997 (now a family of four), where he established a high-quality certified (biodynamic, organic and fair trade) coffee-roasting enterprise.

The selection process was hosted at Auroville's Unity Pavilion, a large building designed for collective events. It consists of a big open hall that fits 250 people, which is also used for general meetings, and another smaller enclosed space, The Hall of Peace, which is regularly used for collective meditations. On the glass double doors that lead into the main hall were posted the profiles of all those who were attending the selection process. Once inside, I soon noticed the beauty of the set-up: there were elegant flower arrangements and small, low tables surrounded by cushions on the floor for people to sit on. At a welcome desk, each participant was asked to pick a token, which determined the table you were to sit at, and a bookmark. The tokens were small square laminated photographs of flowers, identified by The Mother's spiritual names for them – she gave spiritual names to hundreds of flowers, based on what she perceived to be their divine message or essence. The bookmarks were a collection of the 12 qualities of The Mother's symbol: on one side, the name of the quality; on the reverse, a quotation by The Mother on that particular quality. I picked mine at random – the quality Peace and the flower message To Know How to Listen – and made my way to my designated table, identifiable by corresponding, larger versions of the flower photographs.

Each table also had folders with *A Dream, The Auroville Charter* and *To Be a True Aurovilian* – the three reference documents of Auroville, all written by The Mother (1954, 1968, 1971) (see Appendices A, B and C, respectively) – and in the ATDC selection process, documentation of its recent restructure. At my table, I found Alina, a member of the Auroville Council whom I knew, already seated. "We have to relook at the selection process", says Alina, before we even started; "Last time it was such a bumpy road, so hard."

Embodying spiritually prefigurative states

At 9 am on the first day, the facilitation team – a French man in his 60s and two middle-aged Indian women, each Aurovilian – used Tibetan chimes to indicate the beginning of the selection process. They stood in silence for quite a while, a couple of minutes perhaps, until the room fell quiet. Then, one of the women started, saying: "So, the future of Auroville is in silence, when all is contained in silence." The second followed on with: "Let's all in our own ways try to touch the silence for a minute." Finally, the third facilitator concluded with: "Maybe silence can be there for three days – that's our idea. That we don't forget the silence."

While they were speaking, I found myself triggered by the scripted spiritual tone – something that would emerge as an issue for some participants throughout the process, though others appreciated it – even though the proposition was one that I very much connected with. What followed, however, was a beautiful atmosphere of silence in the room, the kind that is hard to describe in words to an audience that is not accustomed to instances of religious or spiritual silence. It is a silence that is not just the absence of sound but one of palpable presence. Some people closed their eyes, while others kept them open. It was a precious moment to me, to be able to create and share that atmosphere collectively – while I had often experienced this in Auroville, such as the Awareness Through the Body session highlighted earlier, I never had in the context of a political, collective decision-making process.

Reportedly, Occupy Wall Street General Assembly facilitators also used moments of silence and short meditation, which 'became more common as the occupation continued, and challenges intensified'(Rowe, 2015), something that points to the strategic use of such practices. In the remainder of this section, I will highlight the specific role of 'silent presence keepers', which were present in the selection processes, a spiritually prefigurative counterpart to that of 'vibes-watchers' in social movement consensus decision-making forums, such as Occupy Wall Street.

Vibes-watchers are members of the facilitation team whose role it is to help address unproductive and inequitable process dynamics in assemblies, for example: noting that people are getting tired and frustrated, and suggesting a break; pointing out that there has been an unpleasant shift in the tone of the conversation; or highlighting gender or race biases in the involvement of participants (Graeber, 2013). Rather than calling out participants on unhealthy dynamics, silent presence keepers act as embodied anchors and reminders of the spiritualization Aurovilians aspire to.

They sit in Auroville's collective decision-making forums (general meetings, working group meetings and the selection process), embodying silence – silence not as in the absence of sound but as a spiritual practice of quieting the activity of the individual ego (thoughts, emotional reactions and impulses) in order to connect with, and become a channel and anchor for, a higher consciousness (Vidal, 2018). This is fundamental to the understanding of what an Aurovilian is called to do: 'Often we are pressed to acknowledge that as Aurovilians we are asked to purge ourselves of our limitations, purifying our intentions, becoming transparent and profoundly reflective and then only can we touch upon the truth that lays behind the decisions we are asked to make' (Roy, 2014).

However, it bears noting that the effectiveness of silent presence keeping has been contested in Auroville. Members of one working group stated that while they could see a personal value for the individual practising silent presence keeping among them, they did not experience a tangible contribution for the group deriving from their presence, and even felt uncomfortable by the attendance of someone who they perceived as entirely disengaged from their process.

While the role of silent present keeper is now a mandated one for Auroville's participatory working groups, some develop additional ways to support this interiorized dimension. The Auroville Council adopted 'The 6 agreements',[2] a protocol of practices that prompt a more spiritualized state during discussions, such as taking a full breath before speaking, listening and speaking to 'the centre' – as experienced spiritually – and empowering anyone to invite silence at any time, used as an opportunity for people to reconnect spiritually (Noubel, 2013). "We put a lot of attention and care in our posture", one Auroville Council member said when the team were presenting themselves at the selection process; "We ask ourselves: are we emotionally challenged? Do we have assumptions? Judgements? We put lots of care to create a conscious space."

While some community members applauded the Auroville Council's use of such spiritually conscious practices, others were more critical. Similarly to the observation made about silence presence keeping, they questioned whether such practices benefited the community at large by translating into more efficient processes and better decisional outcomes, or only the personal well-being of Auroville Council team members. Such doubts about the instrumentality of spiritual practices were expressed throughout the selection process.

Prompting strategic spirituality

Both selection processes included a variety of spirituality-based practices that were used instrumentally to inform participation and not necessarily, or exclusively, to induce a spiritually centred state. These were always based on material from The Mother: clauses of *The Auroville Charter*; other statements she had made about Auroville; or the 12 qualities she had defined as essential to living a spiritually evolved life.

In the opening session of the first selection process, a facilitator guided us through one such exercise: "Let us imagine that there is something like the Divine Consciousness" – an intentionally ironic rhetorical proposition given that Auroville is based on this assumption – "Imagine it is looking at everything we are doing, thinking ... everything that we are, individually and collectively. How does the Divine Consciousness want me to be her willing servitor?" The prompt is drawn from the first clause of *The Auroville Charter* in which The Mother writes that 'to live in Auroville, one must be a willing servitor of the divine consciousness' (The Mother, 1968). The facilitator invited us to concentrate on this question, specifically in relationship to our participation in the selection process, and then to pick a bookmark of the 12 qualities (also referred to as 'powers') of The Mother at random. We were to reflect and share our response to this quality at our tables, being guided by three questions, displayed on the PowerPoint presentation:

Q1: 'Do you feel the Power of the Divine Consciousness has made a good choice?' If Yes, move on to Q2 and Q3.
Q2: 'What does it tell you about your aspiration to participate in the Interface Team?'
Q3: 'Can it help you to contribute meaningfully to the Interface Team?'

As we went to pick our cards, I was touched by the quality of the reflective and collective silence. Some people seemed to be genuinely keen to go through this spiritually reflective exercise, others to be just going through with it and a few protesting by not participating in it. "I don't play card games", said someone at our table, sarcastically. "It's just too much", said the executive of a large commercial unit, to whom I later asked why she had not participated: "I was sitting at a table and had to do stuff completely unrelated to the selection – journaling about the qualities. I don't understand why we can't just vote." Those who did participate, however, seemed to be informed in their positionality in the process by the exercise, which was also undertaken in the second selection process. The following ethnographic account is drawn from both processes.

"I picked Gratitude", said Colette, a middle-aged woman who had told me earlier that she was nervous about being here because she did not want to be selected, having already served on Auroville's working groups. "I feel grateful there will be people to do the job–", she said with a smile, as we all laughed, "and I can be passive, rather than active. I feel more comfortable about being here now." I shared that I had picked 'Sincerity' and that I felt relief because while I had no intention of being selected, I was worried that I might feel called to. "I picked 'Surrender'", said a young Indian woman who was still in her Newcomer process; "I just closed my eyes and asked the Divine to organize my life the way it wants because I'm feeling like I already have a lot of commitments." After we exchanged in our subgroups, one of the facilitators invited anyone who wished to do so to share their experience with the group at large. One woman who was considering joining a team shared that her card was 'Aspiration' and that she really felt it was enough to contribute meaningfully. Another said that his card was 'Progress' and he felt "the need to make inner progress for this work, that I am willing to do." Clearly, there was a strong tendency to recontextualize participation within a spiritual perspective.

As the selection processes progressed, similar exercises were used strategically to inform how participants related to specific areas of work of Auroville's working groups, with mixed responses. A key point of frustration was that spirituality-centred activities were focused on when concerns pertaining to the design of the process were not satisfactorily addressed. A series of case-study exercises of ATDC issues undertaken on the first day of its dedicated selection process is explored in the next section to illustrate this emphasis on, and tension with, spirituality-focused political practice.

Spirituality and participatory politics

After the initial collective moment of silence and individual activity of drawing of a quality, the facilitators presented our agenda for the three days of the selection process – a mix of individual presentations, subgroup exercises and introspective work on the first two days, and the team selection on the third day. One of the facilitators read a quote from The Mother – the opening lines of her address for the founding of Auroville, broadcast live on *All India Radio* on 28 February 1968: 'Greetings from Auroville to all men of goodwill. Are invited to Auroville all those who thirst for progress and aspire to a higher and truer life' (Satprem, 1981: 65). He looked around the room, and said: "This is our common ground – I don't know if anybody disagrees." Nobody responded; the room felt quiet and contemplative. The facilitators then presented our first group exercise: we were to discuss a mock town-planning issue at our table and then share a proposal for it with the room at large.

I was surprised that there was no presentation of the ATDC's mandate and scope of work, or of its new structure, which had led to this very selection process. The introduction had been exclusively focused on spiritual positioning. Prior to the selection process, I had expected to receive preparatory materials by email, specifically, the community-ratified documents outlining the expectations and parameters of the new team. While they were provided on the day, I found that many people in the room were unfamiliar with the material, including the facilitators. I was not the only person in the room who found this concerning: one of the existing ATDC members raised his hand, saying: "I have been here ten years. At which point can I express experience? I don't see it in your programme", a request that the facilitators did not respond to right away.

After the exercise, several Aurovilians who had served on the ATDC or had been involved in its restructure remarked that the Selection Committee needed to be briefed for such an exercise to be worthwhile: "They need to participate with information, not opinion", exhorted an architect who had been on the restructure team; "I was doubting if this would be practical; I was even doubting coming", said a participant who eventually left the process; "I would have liked a presentation from the ATDC: targets, difficulties – they know better than any of us! They could have made some *practical* recommendations."

A presentation of the ATDC had not been programmed, and we continued with spiritualized iterations of the same exercise the facilitators had planned. The facilitators asked each group to revisit their issue in light of one of The Mother's quotes: "If the growth of consciousness were considered as the principal goal of life, many difficulties would find their solution." We were prompted to notice what changed within us and our perception of the situation. Following a period of individual reflection, we each went on to share our insights within our subgroups. I remember feeling stumped in terms of how fostering a growth of consciousness could be facilitated to address the issue we had been working on. A current member of the Auroville Council sitting at my table said: "A change of consciousness can be very small; it doesn't have to be big. ... A group can commit to do that. It's not just good or important; it's *necessary*. If we don't, we are doing the same thing as everywhere else." At another table, I heard someone else say: "But there is no reason to just rely on the growth of consciousness; we can also use common sense; we can also *work*." These two comments portray the crux of the issue: focusing on the spiritual can either distract from strategic action or inform, and perhaps transform, it. Attempting the latter is critical to Auroville's spiritually prefigurative project, and in the next activity, a more practical attempt at infusing Auroville's ideals into the governance of the community's issues was proposed, with continued mixed responses and results.

Engaging with the Auroville Charter

"I am a bit shy about proposing the next exercise", says one of the facilitators, his upper body curling back, seemingly withdrawing from us, while the characteristically playful sparkle in his eye and smile ready to erupt remained undeterred. "I am afraid that many people will 'grrrrr ...'", he says, imitating frustrated annoyance. The *Auroville Charter* is projected on the screen (see Figure 5.2). "I cannot resist the temptation to read it out loud", says the facilitator; "I hope you don't mind." Nobody says anything. I find it a bit heavy-handed. I love the *Auroville Charter*, and I am absolutely for making it central and applicable to all undertakings in Auroville; it is the hint of a proselytizing tone that is triggering me.

After reading the *Auroville Charter*, he poses the prompt for the exercise we are to undertake: "How can the first article of the *Charter* be a framework to guide the [ATDC's] terms of reference and detailed development plan?" Within the same breath, he defends the proposed exercise, saying: "As long as we don't make the *Charter* a practical tool, we will not make it." I notice two of the architects of the terms of reference looking at each other, eyes

Figure 5.2: Scan of the original *Auroville Charter*, handwritten by The Mother

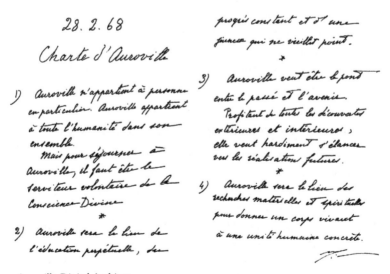

Source: Auroville Digital Archives.

wide with frustrated disbelief. "What is this question?", one of them asks, recalcitrantly, belying the perceived futility of such an exercise in light of the ongoing lack of information provided on the terms of reference and detailed development plan.

The facilitator continues on to explain the exercise: we are to now re-examine the issue we have been working on at our small tables, with the first article of the *Charter* as a point of reference: 'Auroville belongs to nobody in particular. Auroville belongs to humanity as a whole. But to live in Auroville, one must be a willing servitor of the divine consciousness' (The Mother, 1968). The exercise seemed to have varying degrees of success. "In our issues of donations, the *Charter* is the ideal reference document", is the report from one table working on conditions under which to accept donations to the community. "The first point of the *Charter* is not applied here!", someone from another table, working on the issue of privately owned land in Auroville's city plan, exclaimed heatedly. "If we don't apply it to *us*, we cannot apply it to the villages", he continued, referring to the fact that we could not ask non-Aurovilians to sell or donate their land to Auroville if community members were not doing so either. This was revelatory of a greater issue with spiritualized governance in Auroville, as articulated by another participant in the second selection process: that it could not be the exclusive responsibility of the working groups to ensure that Auroville progressed according to its ideals; rather, all Aurovilians were responsible for acting as conscious citizens in order to create a spiritual polity.

The exercise thus revealed a range of responses to the attempted articulation between the ideals of the *Auroville Charter* and the governance of the community in practice. While these ideals were able to offer clarity and guidance in some cases, agency was disabled in scenarios in which present situations so contradicted with them that participants struggled to envisage how the *Auroville Charter* could possibly, practically, be realized within these conditions. Yet, many chose to attend the selection processes to address this gap between ideals and realities on the ground. It is to their motivations that we turn next.

Spiritual motivations for process participation

A core component of the selection process is individual presentations by each of the participants. These are short, only a couple of minutes long for each person, and there is no set format or questions they have to address. In the processes I attended, some people chose to highlight their professional experience, education or specific agendas they had relating to their candidacy for a working group. Others simply expressed that they felt a spiritual 'calling' to work on the team, and some had been nominated by others and were curious to see if they might feel called to join a team during the course of the selection process. Among the candidates were people who had no previous or even related experience of administration, or expertise in the areas of work of any of the working groups, and people who did. This broad divergence in backgrounds and motivations reveals the success of the participatory ideals and accessibility of the selection process, and while some participants with no prior relevant experience were sometimes selected, there was overall dissatisfaction with the lack of a qualified cohort of candidates to choose from.

"I felt something inside that called me forward. I don't know exactly what it is, what I'll bring. ... I have the ability to learn", was the extent of the individual presentation of one participant who ended up being selected. One of my peers, who had been selected in a previous process, said that she had attended it because she was nominated, though when she was first notified of this by the Residents' Assembly Service, she told them they must have called the wrong person. She said she knew very little about Auroville's structure and administration but accepted the working group membership she was selected for and learned on the job. Quite a few people shared similar stories during the selection processes I attended, expressing that they unexpectedly chose to take up working group posts for the experience of serving on one.

Many participants who did have a significant breadth of relevant experience for joining an Auroville working group did not highlight this in their presentations, expressing instead their commitment to the community and its ideals, often visibly moved. One such candidate, a woman in her 60s who had served the community in many capacities, simply said, "I got nominated, and I care for this community a lot. ... I come from a point of service ... my heart is very strong for this evolving experiment", with humility and sweetness.

Where people specifically raised the ideals of Auroville in their personal presentations, these were often linked to dissatisfaction with how these were articulated in practice in Auroville or facilitated by a given group. "I am interested in ideals; I am an idealistic man", said one candidate interested in joining the FAMC, Vincent, who had been researching and formulating proposals for economic reform in Auroville; "I propose myself as someone ... who *really* works on new steps towards alternative economy." Along the same lines, another participant – an outgoing member of the Auroville Council and executive of one of Auroville's most successful enterprises – said: "I am willing to help the FAMC as a resource person to help it align with our ideals, which I feel is not currently the case."

During the ATDC selection process, one candidate – among the few with professional town-planning experience – expressed that she was "frustrated and fascinated, again and again", by the issue of planning in Auroville, which she said was about "collective growth and development to come to a new consciousness, not about building a city as quickly as possible". Another said she came to Auroville 20 years ago "to build the city" but was "not interested to build a city that is beautiful with no spirituality"; both comments pointed to the perceived lack of centrality of spiritual development in the current town-planning process and a desire to address it.

Besides ideals, some participants mentioned The Mother as a source of inspiration for their desire or willingness to serve on Auroville's working groups. One candidate for the ATDC said their interest was, "To serve Mother by developing the city", referring to the city plan that The Mother had commissioned an architect to design; in her presentation, my mother said she was willing to serve on the FAMC because "the economy Mother wanted to manifest is close to my heart".

Perhaps contrary to an outsider's expectations, evoking The Mother can be contentious in the Auroville context, for doing so is sometimes perceived as instrumental to legitimizing personal views and agendas. Some hesitate to make explicit reference to The Mother in public life and governance in Auroville for fear of portraying a fetishized relationship with her, which sits uncomfortably with Auroville's self-understanding of being a 'divine anarchy' that bases itself on non-prescriptive individual and collective spiritual development. This tension came to the fore in the second selection process in response to the use of quotations and recordings of The Mother by the facilitation team, scenes of which are depicted in the next section.

Relating with spiritual legacy: recordings of The Mother

On Sunday morning, the third and last day of the first selection process, one of the facilitators opened a session by reading a quotation of The Mother from a slide of the PowerPoint presentation: "The future of the earth depends on a change of consciousness." He then turns to us and says, "We know this phrase", with a hint of affected complicity. He presses on the PowerPoint pointer and another line of the quote appears: "So, wake up and collaborate. Blessings." Smiling contentedly, he comments on how straightforward The Mother is in saying, "So, wake up and collaborate" and how she then softens it with, "Blessings". I had not felt as triggered that time, but clearly others had because I get passed a note from a friend of mine who is sitting at my table: 'Nirmala says we should all say "Amen" or "Hallelujah" at the end of this sermon…', the note reads. I smile at what I assume is just a joke, thinking to myself that we are all just exhausted and people's patience is wearing thin.

However, when the facilitator next tries to play a recording of The Mother speaking, one of the participants, Loki, promptly walks up and interrupts him, saying something in his ear. I am surprised, both at the rather bold intervention and because the participant is someone I see regularly at the Sri

Aurobindo Ashram in Pondicherry. For this reason, I do not expect him to be uncomfortable at the proposition of listening to The Mother. I too am feeling really uneasy about it, however. "I'm hearing it sounds like Sunday church", says the facilitator. The room is tense. The facilitation team call for a tea break, presumably to confer about what to do next.

When we come back, a second facilitator is ready to play the recording. "But it's going to be a problem for Loki", says the first, out loud to the room. "A problem for a lot of people, actually", another participant announces, in a heavy tone. "Is it such a big deal?", the second facilitator asks, addressing the selection committee at large. Others in the room say, "No, no – go ahead." Some seem genuinely interested in listening to the recording; others just want to diffuse the tension. The very short recording is of The Mother's voice, reading out a quotation well known to Aurovilians: 'The world is preparing itself for a big change. Will you help?' (The Mother, 2003c: 180). Somehow, as soon as The Mother's voice enters the room, the atmosphere shifts to an intensely concentrated receptivity. "That was the year I arrived: 1970", says an older Aurovilian woman sitting next to me; "This is really significant for me." Not a single person raises a concern, and there is no further collective discussion of either the interruption to, or the experience of, listening to the recording. After a quiet pause, we carry on with a consensus-based selection of the final roster of candidates willing to take on a working group role.

In the second selection process, the facilitators project a YouTube video of The Mother – 'The Mother talks about total Surrender' (Jzartl, 2011) – halfway through the actual selection, in which it was proving to be very challenging to find consensus on the candidates. The video is actually an audio recording of The Mother speaking, while a transcript scrolls across a still photograph of her. One of the facilitators starts by announcing that the video is 6:30 minutes and that she will stop at 1:30 minutes, at which point, we can ask her to continue it if we would like it to go on. I am guessing that this bid for consent is based on the contentious response to playing a recording of The Mother in the previous selection process.

I am a bit nervous, given this experience, but no one remonstrates. We are not the same group of people as last time, though many are attending both processes. A beautiful, silent receptivity descends upon the room as the video plays. We are all very present, sort of entranced, utterly silent. As the facilitator readies herself to pause the video at 1:30 minutes, many people speak up spontaneously, asking her to carry on. At the end, someone sitting next to me says, "Thank you." Again, the response is unexpected to me, coming from that person. How we each relate to The Mother is, by and large, a private experience in the community.

Just like in the first selection process, I felt distinctly uneasy before the recording of The Mother was played, but I am moved both by The Mother's message, which I had never heard, and by the collective state of the room as we listen to it all together. I had only ever experienced something similar at the amphitheatre of the Matrimandir (the spiritual centre of Auroville), where a recording of The Mother reading the *Auroville Charter* is played each year on the anniversary of the community's founding. For a concentrated moment, one can feel a conscious, collective connection with the deeper, spiritual purpose and aspiration of our community. To embody such a shared and spiritually concentrated state in the midst of a collective decision-making process was revelatory, to me, of the already-existing spiritualized polity we were attempting to prefigure. Yet, outside of these moments reserved to spirituality, it was difficult to connect with its underlying presence and potential among us. As reviewed earlier, attempts at strategically informing the process and its outcomes with spiritual prompting had mixed results. Beyond this, many participants felt frustrated and disheartened because these overlooked, and thus failed to address, issues with the design and facilitation of the process itself. While the YouTube video of The Mother was played during the final consensus-based selection and seemed to successfully induce a spiritually receptive and centred state, carrying out this selection was challenging due to a lack of consensus on, and clarity of, the process itself, which made it difficult and frustrating for many.

Spiritual practice and political praxis: a few concluding observations

This embodied account of Auroville's selection process reveals the integration of two, sometimes interrelated, categories of spiritual activities. The first includes practices that induce the embodiment of spiritually centred states, such as that of silent presence keeping or listening to spiritual recordings of The Mother. The second consists of exercises that utilize spirituality strategically to inform perceptions, decisions and outcomes. Both were openly contested in the course of the two selection processes I attended. Whereas some Aurovilians welcomed and encouraged the inclusion of explicitly spiritual practices in such forums, there was significant doubt, criticism and even objection to this, which seems to have been due to two key reasons.

One is that these practices did not seem to be relevant to the task at hand, a sentiment that was largely fomented by the lack of practical and strategic guidance and information, which exacerbated the casting of spiritually focused activities as disconnected from realities on the ground. Beyond this, the very facilitation of spiritual activities was problematic for some because it was perceived as imposing certain ways of relating to Auroville's spiritual legacy – notably, quotations and recordings of The Mother – that went against the individually defined exploration it upholds. Both the activities that sought to induce spiritually centred states and the ones that sought to strategically influence various aspects of the process did have some level of success, however, and the very participation and candidature of Aurovilians in the selection process was significantly linked to a spiritually informed 'calling'. That the participation and candidature of Aurovilians in the selection process was significantly linked to spiritually informed attitudes and motivations (see Clarence-Smith, 2019a) is a counter to the critique that spirituality renders individuals apolitical (see Žižek, 2001).

Previous scholarship has pointed to the potential of spiritual practices – whether embodied or contemplative – for developing new subjectivities and relational capacities that could significantly facilitate collective decision-making processes in political forums (see Chari, 2016; Litfin, 2018). When adopted within these forums, spiritual practices could generate or resuscitate these experiences of subjectivity, and thus act as strategic, micropolitical interventions towards facilitating the dispositions necessary for successfully engaging in prefigurative macropolitics (see Connolly, 2002; Rowe, 2016). In this chapter, we have seen that spiritually centring practices were used within the Auroville selection process as strategic micropolitical interventions towards engaging in and sustaining an overarching, spiritually prefigurative political process (see Connolly, 2002; Rowe, 2016).

This case study reveals an additional way in which spirituality can be strategically used towards facilitating a spiritually prefigurative political praxis. The community's spiritual ideals were applied as instrumental prompts to frame and inform the actual content of the decision making towards prefiguring these. While it is important to note that an emphasis on such practices seems to be correlated with a failure to provide practical guidance – echoing the criticism that a focus on the spiritual causes an elision of worldly concerns – this attempted articulation between spiritual ideals and actual governance did have varying levels of success. Regarding the concerns raised by Aurovilians related to their own selection process, a review was undertaken shortly after the two described in this chapter were completed, and an amended framework was ratified by the community at large. The design of the process has continued to evolve, each selection process bringing out new challenges and opportunities for improvement.

In examining the spiritualization of a collective decision-making process in the intentional community of Auroville, this chapter builds on scholarship that highlights the significance of embodied spiritual practices in prefigurative political praxis and the potential for spiritually informed world views and subjectivities to prompt, inform and sustain such praxis (Wilson, 2014; Brown, 2016; Chari, 2016; Rowe, 2016; Johnson and Kraft, 2018; Litfin, 2018). While the prevalent 'taboo on the notion of interior life' (Morton, 2015: 251) present in both left-wing and academic circles sidelines this spiritual dimensionality, indigenous movements like Protect Mauna Kea or

Stand with Standing Rock, or the practice of intentional communities like Auroville, Damanhur and Findhorn, reflect its centrality. Even left-wing social movements like Occupy Wall Street highlighted the importance of transformation at personal, collective and world levels – 'a peace-full person first, a peace-full collective second leads to a peace-full earth' (Writers for the 99%, 2012: 92) – integrating practices of meditation to cultivate this understanding 'of the connection between personal transformation practices and social transformation' (Writers for the 99%, 2012: 88). Indeed scholars are increasingly pointing to how mindfulness practices are often integrated into environmentalist and social justice movements (Kabat-Zinn 2013; Berila, 2016; Yang and Willis, 2017).

Auroville's overarching aim is to prefigure the spiritual vision of Integral Yoga, a vision manifest from the practice of fusing the spiritual and material realms of existence, including societal realities, with the aim of uplifting the latter. On a vision level, this responds to the criticism of spirituality being inevitably (and in some spiritual traditions, intentionally) disconnected from ground realities. While the effectiveness of this practice of integration is partial in the context of Auroville's political practice, I remain curious about its potential to evolve. That the community is committed to continuing to mature the latter is evident, for example, recent meetings have dedicated up to half an hour for spiritual centring before discussions begin. In Chapter 6, we will explore another aspect of spiritually prefigurative politics in the Auroville context: how the spiritually inspired economic ideals of Auroville feature in the administration of the community, specifically, in the context of one of its economic working groups.

PART III

Economy

6

'No Exchange of Money'? The Development of Auroville's Communal Economy

Introduction

> [I]t is questions ... of the proper organisation and administration of the economic life of the society which are preparing the revolutions of the future.
>
> Sri Aurobindo, 1997: 449

It was clear from the inception of Auroville that its economic organization would be critical for prefiguring a spiritualized society. This grounding of a utopian project in the material conditions of life is characteristic of what Marxist utopian scholars define as 'real' (Wright, 2010) or 'concrete' (Bloch, 1986) utopias. To this day, the topic of how to prefigure such an 'Auroville economy' is alive, being a source of both aspiration and frustration, and wrought with challenges, not only legal and financial but also of competing visions and approaches to economic administration in Auroville. Here, we will explore how the community's founding economic ideals continue to galvanize, underpin and inform the emergence and evolution of Auroville's communal economic framework, institutions and policies to prefigure an alternative embedded in a mainstream capitalist context by engaging in a critical and reflexive process.

We will begin with understanding the founding economic ideals for Auroville and the roots of Auroville's economic organization in that of the Sri Aurobindo Ashram, and then investigate the early history of the community's economy and how its communal character and administration has (d) evolved over more recent years, and under which pressures. Specifically, I will be drawing on autoethnographic insights into the management of Auroville's 'central fund', or municipal budget, and the 'Maintenance' (or economic support) of Aurovilians to explore attempts to balance collective and individual provisioning, as per the community's socio-economic ideals.

Revealing the means and praxis of prefiguring the community's socio-economic ideals, including the ongoing efforts and trials faced by fellow community members in doing so, this rich case study will be particularly relevant for practices of participatory budgeting and non-monetary forms of provision, universal basic services, and basic income policy programmes.

Sri Aurobindo Ashram: the roots of Auroville's economic organization

Auroville did not start with a blank slate in terms of its economic imaginary; The Mother had already created a unique economic unit out of the Sri Aurobindo Ashram in Pondicherry, in which she prefigured a model for economic organization congruent with the ideals of a spiritualized society of Integral Yoga, as well as spiritualized approaches to economic activity. This experience formed the basis of her economic vision for Auroville and was instrumental in the formulation of the Auroville economy, continuing to inform its development to this day.

Unlike other ashrams, in which members primarily engage in meditation, devotional practices, the study of sacred scripture or acts of charitable service – and that rely almost exclusively on donations for their subsistence – under The Mother's direction, members of the Sri Aurobindo Ashram developed and managed numerous enterprises as 'departments' of the ashram. These include wood and steel workshops (Harpagon Workshop), handmade paper and incense factories (The Handmade Paper Factory, Auroshikha), an interior design and furniture firm (Auroform and Aurofurn), a printing press, an Ayurvedic clinic and a cosmetics laboratory and shop (Laboratoire Senteurs and Fleurs en Flacon) (see Sri Aurobindo Ashram, no date[a]; MiraAura, 2002). Most were founded in Pondicherry the 1940s, 1950s and 1960s, and are still in operation today, recognizable throughout the city by their 'ashram grey' wall exteriors (and the display of The Mother's and Sri Aurobindo's symbols in the signage, as well as photographs in the interiors, though the latter are also used by non-ashramite shop-owners who are nonetheless devotees). They were founded based on the skills and interests of ashramites, whose pursuit The Mother encouraged as a form of Karma Yoga[1] – of work according to one's nature and as an offering to the Divine.

Income generated from these enterprises sustains the ashram and its members (though not exclusively, as the ashram also receives donations), each of whom work in one of the Ashram's departments, which also include free services for ashramites and ashram life. Ashramites working in any department, whether a service or a business, do not derive a direct monetary income from their work; instead, they are housed, fed and cared for by the ashram, receiving a monthly bundle of basic commodities (that is, clothing, toiletries and pocket money) – called 'Prosperity' – and can engage in any of the numerous complimentary educational, artistic, cultural and sportive activities organized by the ashram.

'Concrete utopia': the prefigurative rationale for Auroville's economy

The economic organization of the Sri Aurobindo Ashram is a seed form of the one The Mother seemed to envisage for Auroville. Clearly, she considered that a new form of economic organization was necessary to facilitate the spiritual and material emancipation of individuals, as well as the relationships of solidarity between them, in order to create a conscious, harmonious society. The Mother never comprehensively defined how Auroville should function; its premise was to be a spiritually prefigurative experiment in conscious evolution, and forms of collective organization would emerge out of this process and continue to develop alongside it. They could not be anticipated and should not be prescribed; on the contrary, space for them to manifest, unfettered, should be safeguarded. For this reason, The Mother (2003a: 261, 266) insisted on there being no fixed rules in Auroville and that its organization 'must be flexible and progressive' (The Mother, 1977: 71).

Interestingly, while Marx offered an insightful critique of capitalism, he did not detail how a communist system would function, by virtue of the same reasoning that The Mother did not for Auroville: one could not anticipate how a society with a heightened level of collective consciousness (the communist project) or a heightened collective level of consciousness (the Auroville project) would choose to do so. The point was not to predetermine and prescribe how a future society of emancipated individuals would organize but for it to develop in tandem with its members. This is consistent with the Marxist utopian philosopher Ernst Bloch's (1986: 146) insistence that 'utopian' does not describe a perfect and fixed state but, rather, a dynamic function, the role of which is to reach into the 'Novum' – the entirely new – informed by a potentiality latent in the present. His redefinition enables us to recognize an alternative utopian rationale in the refusal to prescribe new societies, one that stands in direct contrast to the 'blueprint' approach of the utopian social theorists that were Marx's contemporaries (notably, Etienne Cabet, Henri de Saint-Simon and Charles Fourier) and other utopian thinkers before them, as early as Plato.

Marx and Engels condemned these abstract and theoretical utopias for not being grounded in reality, for not taking into account the material conditions of the time and for therefore being unrealistic and futile – a common criticism of utopianism (Marx and Engels, 1848; Engels, 1880; Paden, 2002). By contrast, both Marx and The Mother focused on creating the catalytic conditions for the societies they envisioned to be able to develop. While Marx himself would have shuddered to think of the communist project being referred to as utopian due its contemporary conceptualization – the

103

same reason Aurovilians cringe at our community being referred to as a 'utopia' – Marxist scholars have since theorized 'concrete' (Bloch, 1986) and documented 'real' (Wright, 2010) utopias, that is, prefigurative projects that exist within the limitations and potentialities of the present.

The fact that The Mother showed a keen interest in economic organization, both at the Sri Aurobindo Ashram and for Auroville, demonstrates the importance she lent to grounding these prefigurative experiments in spiritualized society in material conditions as 'real' and 'concrete' utopias. Economy is an area in which she gave not only broad directives for Auroville (the three founding texts of the community, *A Dream*,[2] *The Auroville Charter* and *To Be a True Aurovilian* [The Mother, 1954, 1968, 1971], all include elements of her economic ideals for the township) but also elements of specific arrangements, though it is important to note that these were offered in response to questions from ashramites and early Aurovilians, not as part of a predetermined blueprint (see The Mother, 1977, 2003c). These would serve not only to concretize the project materially but also to facilitate the spiritual evolution of consciousness that Sri Aurobindo and The Mother perceived was already under way; this 'anticipatory' quality of reaching for the 'Not-Yet-Become' while rooted in the present characteristic of Bloch's (1986) conception of 'concrete' utopianism. It is to these economic ideals that we turn next.

Economic ideals for Auroville

The broad-strokes principles that can be gleaned from The Mother's various statements on the topic are that Auroville's economy should be communal, with no private property and no exchange of money between community members, each of whom would contribute to the collective – in one of three ways, 'work, kind[3] or money' (The Mother, 2003a: 261) – and whose basic needs would, in turn, be provided for by the community. Just like the Sri Aurobindo Ashram, Auroville would develop enterprises to finance the project (The Mother, 2003a: 261–7; Auroville, 2017).

Not only did these guidelines have as their objectives to assure a socio-economic organization that would foster solidarity among community members, but they would also support the spiritual evolution of individuals. The absence of private property in Auroville would assist in compelling individuals to seek inspiration and reward for their work and action elsewhere than in worldly gains and satisfaction; in *A Dream*, The Mother (1954) describes 'a place where the needs of the spirit and the concern for progress would take precedence over the satisfaction of desires and passions, the search for pleasure and material enjoyment'. Out of the three ways Aurovilians would contribute economically to the community (work, kind or money), work was the form that The Mother (1971) described in *To Be a True Aurovilian* as necessary for their own 'inner discovery', for it would provide a field of action in which people could discover and develop their own potentialities.

For Aurovilians to be able to choose work best suited for this personal growth, it had to be divorced from the necessity of earning a living, which is why she envisioned a community in which the basic needs of the members would be provided for collectively. In *A Dream*, The Mother (1954) describes a society in which 'work would not be a way to earn one's living but a way to express oneself and to develop one's capacities and possibilities while being of service to the community as a whole, which, for its own part, would provide for each individual's subsistence and sphere of action'. There are obvious parallels here with the argument for a universal basic income, which proposes that all citizens of a nation receive an unconditional stipend, arguing that this would enable many individuals to engage in (more) meaningful work, something that would benefit humanity as a whole (Wright, 2010; Bregman, 2016).

Having a system of collective provisioning would not only ensure that the material conditions for this spiritualization of work would be assured, it would also create economic conditions in which cooperative human relationships could flourish. By supplanting transactions (be these monetized or accounted for through any alternative form of market-based exchange) between Aurovilians, free interactions – free in both senses of the term – could flourish in the community. The Mother envisioned there being no money in Auroville's internal economy (Auroville, 2017), by which she almost undoubtedly meant no form of market-based exchange within the community. This would serve to enable individuals to thrive in society unrestricted by economic barriers and by the pernicious effects on human relationships that result from (often unequal) exchanges conditioned by the market (Wright, 2010: 79). This rationale echoes that of Marx, for whom a key concern was the alienation and competition that arises between people in capitalist societies, in which individuals are not organized as a community (their work not contributing to the community as a whole, nor benefitting them as a member of the community, but instead favouring a bourgeois class), which 'conflicts with the ideal of solidarity with other human beings' (quoted in Haberman and Stevenson, 1998: 132). In *A Dream*, The Mother (1954) imagines:

> Beauty in all its artistic forms, painting, sculpture, music, literature, would be equally accessible to all; the ability to share in the joy it brings would be limited only by the capacities of each one and not by social or financial position. ... In short, it would be a place where human relationships, which are normally based almost exclusively on competition and strife, would be replaced by relationships of emulation in doing well, of collaboration and real brotherhood.

As Sri Aurobindo (1997: 256) previously wrote:

> The aim of its [a spiritualized society's] economics would be not to create a huge engine of production, whether of the competitive or the cooperative kind, but to give men – not only to some but to all men in his highest possible measure – the joy of work according to their own nature and free leisure to grow inwardly, as well as simply a rich and beautiful life for all.

The Mother was clearly aware of the communist project and recognized the parallels between it and the principles of ideal socio-economic organization she began to apply in the Sri Aurobindo Ashram and further envisioned for Auroville, which she said constituted 'a sort of adaptation of the communist system' (The Mother, 1977: 24). She specified that it would be an adaptation because it would eschew what she called the 'spirit of levelling' (The Mother, 1977: 23): a one-size-fits-all system that left no room for diversity in the relationship between the individual and the collective. She was very clear that each person residing in Auroville would participate in the collective, but they would do so according to their capacities; their participation was not something to be 'calculated', and the basic needs of each were to be met, though not 'according to ideas of rights or equality' (The Mother, 1977: 23).

This is, in fact, what Marx had foreseen as the future of communism, captured in the iconic idiom: 'From each according to his ability, to each according to his needs' (quoted in Haberman and Stevenson, 1998: 136). Despite the explicit intention in this statement that the individual's capacity to participate and degree of need would be the decisive lynchpin around which the collective would be organized, early communist states, such as the Soviet Union, established command economies in which what The Mother refers to as 'levelling' was the norm. Auroville has also been challenged by the project of institutionalizing flexible systems, that is, of organizing individuals into a collective without standardizing participation and exchange, and the next section will explore this in detail.

'For All/Pour Tous': collective provisioning for Aurovilians

In the early years of the community, when Auroville was still operating under the aegis of the Sri Aurobindo Society,[4] Aurovilians each received the Prosperity bundle from the Sri Aurobindo Ashram. This constituted a basic modicum of support that was the same for everyone, but individuals could make requests for additional items, and families, of course, were awarded additional amounts according to the number of their children. The first collective provisioning operation of the Auroville community was established

Figure 6.1: Inauguration of the Pour Tous building, 28 February 1974

Source: Anonymous photographer (Auroville Digital Archives).

in 1974 on the suggestion of a community member, Claire Fanning, who wrote to The Mother in 1972, concerned with the existing circulation of money in Auroville and expressing the need for a 'proper channel': 'If Auroville is to function fluently for need and demand without the internal exchange of monies perhaps it is time to create a "proper channel"' (Fanning, 2011). The Mother approved of the idea and offered the name 'For All/Pour Tous', and the Sri Aurobindo Society funded the service (see Figure 6.1).

Aurovilians managing Pour Tous supplemented food grown and products made by the community with purchased goods from ashram departments and the Pondicherry market. These food and sundry items were distributed to all Aurovilians via a weekly basket delivery service along the same lines of Prosperity: equal shares, with exceptions made where needed (see Figure 6.2). There was no exchange of money, as Aurovilians did not directly receive the funds allocated for their needs, which were instead collectively channelled into the Pour Tous Fund.

As I understand it, a confluence of events resulted in a significant shift away from the community's heretofore simplistic collective provisioning system in the 1980s and towards one in which individuals were allocated funds and credit against the fulfilment of certain conditions. Following the passing of The Mother in 1973, the Sri Aurobindo Society attempted to institutionalize her charismatic authority and guidance of the community into ongoing management, which Aurovilians protested. The Sri Aurobindo Society went so far as to illegally withhold donations to Auroville, resulting in legal action and the involvement of the central government in the management

Figure 6.2: Pour Tous baskets

Source: Anonymous photographer (Auroville Digital Archives).

of Auroville in 1980, as decreed in an act of Parliament, the Auroville Emergency Provisions Act 1980. The withholding of funds had thrown the community into a state of economic precarity; its fledgling internal economy was not yet strong enough to sustain all of its members. The content of the community baskets had been meagre even with the financial support of the Sri Aurobindo Society – I heard numerous accounts of Aurovilians present at the time saying that on some occasions, they would look at its contents and wonder how they would make it through the week, feeling thrilled when butter was included.

In 1983, in the face of insufficient funds to provide for all Aurovilians, the community chose to allocate resources only to those who were working for Auroville. This was the founding of the Maintenance system that is still in place today, in which Aurovilians receive a monthly stipend to an account in their name. The decision closely coincided with the granting of government funding to be disbursed to Aurovilians involved in education. A member of the Sri Aurobindo Ashram, Kireet Joshi – a previous officer of the Indian government's premier civil service, the Indian Administrative Service (IAS) – was appointed education advisor to the government of India by then Prime Minister Indira Gandhi in 1976, a post that he held until 1988. In 1983/84, Mr Joshi secured funding from the Indian government for Auroville as an experimental site of Integral Education (the philosophy of education arising from Integral Yoga), founding the SAIIER in Auroville, an entity that continues to receive and disburse the ongoing government grant, along with other donations towards educational research in the community. In 1984, the grant was awarded to educators, which required them having individual accounts in their names for accountability purposes. To avail of this financing, Auroville needed a more complex and individuated structure than that of a 'common pot' that it had used up to then.

The notion of individual accounts was antithetical to the communal ethos and economic ideals of Auroville; the shift from the collective to the individual as the primary locus of economic identity was perceived as a crisis of divergence away from the founding aspiration of a collective life. The transition from centralized provisioning through Pour Tous to the individualized Maintenance system was a challenging one, as it effectively institutionalized a standardized exchange between each community member and the collective through, at least in part, the allocation of money, which for many was – and still is – a contradiction with the founding principles of Auroville's communal economy. On several occasions, I have heard people say, in tones bemoaning and berating, that it is "not an *Aurovilian* system". The change prompted and was accompanied by a period of community-wide seminars, surveys and general meetings centred on a widespread concern with the economic orientation and organization of Auroville, and the aspiration to set up a system that would reflect a continued commitment and development towards the original economic ideals (Thomas and Thomas, 2013).

In the late 1980s, Pour Tous became computerized and each individual member or family unit was given an account in which to deposit funds and encouraged to deposit these in advance of their Pour Tous consumption (Otto Alois, quoted in Thomas and Thomas, 2013: 82). The community basket service soon phased out, with each individual or family paying individually for each item taken. However, it was not to be the end of common pots; a series of others would emerge almost immediately after the Maintenance system was established, which is explored in detail in Chapter 7.

The emergence of Auroville's current economic administration

To mitigate the circulation of money in Auroville in the wake of the shift away from a simple common-pot collective provisioning system to one in which individual community members were directly allocated resources, the community set up a new collective fund in 1991, the Auroville Maintenance Fund,[5] administered by the Financial Service, operative to this day (see Auroville, 2018). Each individual community member or family had their own account at the Financial Service – called a Pour Tous account at first, retaining the name of the original communal fund and provisioning service – into which they could deposit personal funds and through which their Auroville Maintenance was channelled (Otto Alois, quoted in Thomas and Thomas, 2013: 83). All Auroville entities – community members and units – had accounts at the Financial Service, enabling cash-free transfers within the community, which continues to be the norm today.

A communal fund and its mandate were established in June 1989, alongside the Auroville Maintenance Fund administered by the Financial Service. This Central Fund (renamed the 'City Services Budget' in 2008) collected earnings from Auroville units, donations to the community and a standard monthly contribution from each Aurovilian adult[6] to fund Auroville's public sector, referred to in Auroville as the 'Service' sector. There exist several categories of 'services'. Prosperity Services provide for the basic needs[7] of community members, based on The Mother's guiding directives that the basic needs of each would be borne and provided for by the collective. Others, such as Municipal, Administrative, Education & Culture Services, are dedicated to non-commercial community development. Communal funds either fully finance or subsidize the operating costs and provisions made by these services, as well as funding the Maintenances of Aurovilians working in them. By contrast, commercial units directly fund their own operating costs, including the Maintenances of Aurovilians working in the same, since they are income generating.

The 'Economy Group' (reconstituted as the 'Budget Coordination Committee' [BCC] in 2008), a representative group of revolving Aurovilians from various community sectors, was established to manage the budgeting and allocation of the communal fund.[8] Previously, funds were distributed to various sectors and geographical areas of Auroville as decided upon at 'envelopes' community meetings, at which monies were disbursed in envelopes (as there was not yet a financial service with accounts for various Auroville activities).

The exploration from which this system of economic organization initially emerged had several iterations – in 1996, just a few years after it was established, a survey of 1,200 community members specifically asked which services should be part of this centrally supported economy, as well as the conditions for receiving a Maintenance (Thomas and Thomas, 2013: 82). To this day, reforming the collective economic organization of the community so as to reflect its founding economic ideals more closely continues to be a topic of strong interest in the community, with many informal groups of individuals, as well as economic working groups, exploring how to do so.

It is important to note that this topic and challenge was alive prior to the shift of the 1990s as well. One Financial Service executive highlights a general meeting in the early 1980s in which the community had come up with three steps to phase towards a collective economy: "We didn't manage to take the first!", he exclaimed. "There are no shortcuts", he offered as an explanation, "we have to move ourselves", by which he was implying that we have to evolve as individuals in order for a collective shift to happen. "I'm quite busy with that, and I see how hard it is", he added, with a disarming depth of sincerity.[9]

Departures from Auroville's founding communal economic principles

There have been several significant modifications of the economic system described earlier – still in place today – which many feel represent further departures from the founding economic vision and ideals of the community. In 1998, a 33 per cent contribution policy was introduced, whereby all 'commercial units' (the term used to describe Auroville's commercial enterprises) are expected to donate 33 per cent of their net profit to city services unspecified; previously, no percentage was defined and donors were able to specify areas to be funded by their contributions. In 2017, this 33 per cent contribution policy was extended to income-generating services. In the mid-2000s, the Economy Group, faced with budgetary constraints, began requesting certain services to become 'self-supporting'; while they did not operate with the intention of generating a profit, they had to generate enough income to meet their operational costs.[10] In practice, this has resulted in certain services requiring a fixed or scaling contribution from Aurovilians to avail of their provision.[11] Both the 33 per cent contribution policy and the encouraging of self-supporting services have had significant ramifications for Auroville's collective economy and economic solidarity, particularly due to the economic 'policing' they instigate. The following two subsections will explore in detail the issues raised by, and in the implementation of, each, highlighting how the BCC – in charge of their economic administration – sought to navigate the bureaucratization and contradictions that each entailed. This is over the course of my doctoral fieldwork (2017–18), during which I attended BCC meetings as an observer.[12]

The 33 per cent contribution policy: the policing of economic solidarity?

The 33 per cent policy was first established in 1998 to ensure that a reasonable amount was put towards the communal fund by all commercial units, while leaving enough profits – 67 per cent – for the units to be able to contribute to specific projects or reinvest in their own development should they choose to, something that units intent on growing consider to be critical for the long-term prosperity of the community. However, while the 33 per cent policy was introduced as a minimum Central Fund contribution, in practice, few units currently give more, including ones that are widely perceived as being financially able to. The unintended consequence of the policy establishing a practised 'maximum', rather than a minimum, has been decried by several individuals involved in Auroville's economic administration, notably, at a recent general meeting on the new 'Code of conduct' for Auroville units (Auroville Foundation, 2017). One BCC member and commercial unit executive felt that the policy was flawed from the start because it conflicted with The Mother's founding directive that commercial units would contribute all of their 'surplus profit' to the community's Central Fund (Hadnagy, 2005: 21); the fact that it would erode this understanding was thus a predictable outcome. It was not in the scope of my research to explore or verify quantitatively whether, on average, Auroville's commercial units did in fact contribute more to the communal fund before the introduction of the 33 per cent policy. However, qualitative research yielded rich insights into a negative shift in attitudes that accompanied the adoption of this contribution policy on the part of both unit holders and BCC members themselves, who referred to the contribution as a 'tax' and linked the policy to the erosion of goodwill and solidarity.

Prior to the introduction of the policy, commercial unit executives decided independently how much they donated to the communal fund and were able to make 'specified' contributions to designated sectors or activities – a notable example was a partnership in the 1990s between Maroma, one of Auroville's largest units and highest contributors, and Auroville's Farm Group, in which Maroma subsidized Auroville farms to grow and provide free food for the Solar Kitchen.[13] The 33 per cent is an unspecified contribution, and while units are free to make additional specified donations, the practice has by and large disappeared; the only institutionalized carryover is an 'in-kind' (such as food items) contribution that units can make towards educational activities that is deductible from their 33 per cent. That in-kind contributions are restricted to one sector seems contradictory to the ideal of no exchange of money, promoting on the contrary a financialization of Auroville's internal economy, though in recent years, the BCC has been exploring a widening of the in-kind contributions policy.

While commercial unit executives do not contest the role of the BCC as a dedicated community funding allocation body,[14] some reported that they had found it more compelling to form relationships with other Auroville projects by funding their activities directly through specified contributions. "People used to be able to come to us and say: 'Listen, I have a project, can you help me.' We cannot even listen to people with projects anymore", one commercial unit executive said to me, mournfully.[15] Some resent the impersonality with which contributions are now arbitrarily expected of them and administered by a mechanism they feel disenfranchised from:

'They [the BCC] have such a way of processing the money that you give; it's just MIND-blowing ... because you've given this much more, then next year, you have to give based on that and– it's just, it spirals off and ... you sit there and say, "Why am I even doing this?"'[16]

The erasure of mutuality and reciprocity predicated by the bureaucratic deployment of the 33 per cent contribution policy has been corrosive to the fostering and maintaining of a sense of community, eroding what one commercial unit executive said used to be the "joy"[17] of contribution, as well as undermining a feeling of fellowship between unit executives and the BCC. This is not surprising given that the BCC carries out a 'policing' role, requesting the balance sheets of units to calculate the amounts due to the City Services Budget, following up with people who have not contributed the full 33 per cent.

However, BCC members are all too aware of the issues raised by the policy and its implementation – themselves bemoaning the fact that it compels them to act like "tax collectors".[18] The following conversation,[19] sparked by the topic of pending contributions, offers remarkable insight into how they reflect on and resist bureaucratization to safeguard an 'Auroville spirit':

'What is the total pending contributions?', asks Marvin, one of the members.

We look at the spreadsheet projected on the screen in the meeting room.

'Rs. 3.6 crores',[20] someone reads out loud. 'That's the total arrears since 2010. For 2016/2017 [the past financial year], it's 1.5 crores pending.'

Several people utter shocked sounds. I am also quite taken aback. And at the same time, I note that there is no penalty on late contribution.

'We are becoming tax collectors', says Ralph, visibly dismayed. 'I used to be on the Economy Group.[21] People used to give. They should be generous and give. There is a different dynamic [at present]. It's not good. We don't want to go after units. Something is happening to this community regarding contributing. I'm just noting that. It's not good. We will become tax collectors. I have a strong feeling something is wrong.' Getting to know Ralph in the context of BCC meetings had been a gem of a discovery for me, his intelligent and heartfelt dedication to the community and its ideals anchoring what felt to me like a deep, 'Aurovilian' spirit of the group.

'Often, they don't give the minimum contributions', said Narayan, in his characteristically quiet and kind, yet clear, tone. His presence radiated these qualities, which, alongside his competence and humility, reassured me that Auroville's future was in good hands. A young Aurovilian of about my age who had worked in banking in France, he had recently returned to the community with his young family and was working as a resource person for the BCC.

'The more we become tax collectors the more people will try to avoid', says Marvin. '*Without choosing to do it* [be tax collectors], *we are doing it*', he adds, in a stronger tone. 'It's easier for us to have an excel sheet, to calculate the 33 per cent and to ask people to pay. Another option is to meet people and involve them in the decision making. It's more time-consuming, and we cannot do it with a weekly BCC meeting.' After a pause. 'We cannot decide alone. We have to associate everybody.'

'We have to take a step', says Clemence, acquiescing, and I felt relieved that it had all become so human. The vibe felt good – deeper, realer.

'We have to remind the community and unit holders that we are not tax collectors. Units are there to support all of us', says Arundhati, the Auroville Board of Services representative.

'Sometimes, units don't know [that they have pending contributions], then get a big amount for years' worth of arrears', says Praveen, the Auroville Board of Commerce representative. 'This group is lacking competency in sending them clear requests.'

A few of us, myself included, nodded. It sounded very plausible.

'When Solana was here [a community-at-large representative who was born and raised in Auroville], she said a lot of the younger people simply didn't understand clearly', Isabella adds.

'So, we have to make a statement, give some information?', asks Clemence, trying to concretize next steps, with just an undertone of frustration which betrayed the many years she must have spent having these kinds of conversations, only to not see them followed up on.

'Shall we post something in the News and Notes?', asks Arundhati.

'As soon as we do that, an "us and them" is created with the unit holders, and we don't want to do that. It should be a last resort', says Isabella, the BCC secretary.

'It requires *personal relationship*', emphasizes Ralph, the Financial Service representative. 'We just have to *do it*: phone calls to those units.'

'I get all kind of reactions when I contact unit executives', says Narayan, referring to when he first informs them (via email) of their pending contributions. 'People who are happy to pay; people who acknowledge the arrears but don't settle them; people who don't reply … it would help if someone could do a phone follow-up, sometimes they tell you a whole story, it's not easy', he says, uneasily. 'I'm not a fiscal agent. I'm not going to say, "If you don't pay, it'll be an extra 10 per cent." I don't want to do that; I didn't come here [to Auroville] for that.' (Fieldnotes from BCC meeting, 24 August 2017)

Members of the BCC – whose meetings I observed during my doctoral fieldwork in 2017 – certainly did not feel like tax collectors to me. The previous exchange conveys that: despite the institutionalization of economic policies in Auroville, there is another spirit that underlies and informs how the BCC functions, one that ensures that the human – and humane – remains central to it as an Auroville institution. Policies were not indiscriminately considered to be the key referent in addressing a given situation 'objectively'; on the contrary, the subjective and personal aspects of these were routinely discussed and assessed – an administrative practice I like to think of as 'subjectively objective'. It is precisely the subjectivity in this objectivity that ensures that it remains 'Aurovilian' in character, fundamentally flexible, responsive and solidary, which is relevant in the context of increased bureaucratization in Auroville.

These findings may be surprising for some community members, however, who reported at the time that they felt the BCC lacked empathy and understanding in their administrative practice. One commercial unit executive said she wished there were more "heart" behind it,[22] while I found that BCC members internally discussed issues pertaining to fellow community members with a surprising degree of compassion. I offer two points of consideration to account for this discrepancy. The first is that the BCC's communication practices at the time did not accurately reflect and embody its administrative practice – something that has been intentionally improved since. The second is that the very existence of a policy and its deployment – the 'look and feel' of an objective tax alone – in and of itself has a detrimental effect on goodwill, and perhaps even on economic solidarity, within the community. Both have broader implications for developing forms and practices of institutionalization and administration practice, both in Auroville and in other anarchist contexts, that retain a culture of mutuality.

On self-supporting services: the permeation of capitalist logic?

In The Mother's early conceptions of economic provisioning in Auroville, she imagined community-funded services that would meet the basic needs of Aurovilians without charging them individually for these, for this would be key to realizing a society with no exchange of money. In the early years of community life, the Pour Tous service operated this way, and as the community's size and economy grew, so did its service sector, with services being fully or partially funded by the Central Fund (or, as it came to be called, the City Services Budget) based on how much the fund could support, how essential the service was and how many Aurovilians made use of it.

In the mid-2000s, the Economy Group in charge of this budgeting exercise assessed the model of centrally supported services as financially onerous and inefficient, and encouraged a shift towards self-supporting services to address this. Self-supporting services were to operate in the same spirit as centrally funded services, in that they were to meet the basic needs of Aurovilians on a cost-price, not-for-profit basis, though with no support from the City Services Budget. They would have to push operational costs to users, something that partially funded services would also have to resort to, in order to stay afloat.

Doing so is problematic because by asking these services to be income generating forces them to operate on a different economic logic – one in which community members become consumers – causing services to lose their institutional character. Even though they may only be charging the cost price, having Aurovilians individually pay for services rendered goes against the economic ideals of collective and free provisioning, and many community members and service administrators resent this divergence. The practice of charging, alone, can even arouse suspicion as to whether the service is operating at a profit instead of in a true 'spirit of service', to the point that their receiving financial support from the City Services Budget is contested. The BCC was well aware of this 'double standard' – services are meant to provide services free of cost to Aurovilians, yet they are compelled to charge Aurovilians for services rendered because they are not fully funded – and the erosional dynamic it engenders for such services, as seen in the following exchange[23]:

'When we start giving a double standard – you have to be a service but you can bill a little – it starts to go wrong', says Arundhati, the ABS [Auroville Board of Services] representative, and an executive of a fully funded service. 'How do you know what part to bill? If I had to bill, it would be a headache – where do I stop? How much do I take? Shankra Service was *amazing*, it is going wrong because we are asking it to *BILL*. We really have to support the services, but support them *completely* so that they don't have to go into billing things. I really think it is important to take care of all of us, and that is the way we are doing that, with services. So, I find it really hard that we ask services to be self-supporting and then question them.'

'We have a lot of services like this', Praveen adds, in a defeated tone.

'BCC, we are for the *services*; it is our strength. So, each time I see a service die …', Arundhati adds, her voice vibrant with exasperation.

'I so agree with what Arundhati says', Isabella pipes in. 'Once you start charging, it's the end of the service somehow.'

'We have to do something about pure services for Aurovilians', says Ralph, with earnest passion and concern. 'This is the most crucial stuff. We've got to get back there. This dual thing [partially supported services] was a good intention, but it will destroy.'

'Part of our mandate, one of the first things, is to promote an economy without exchange of money', asserts Marvin. 'But we let things go naturally, and the market takes up allocation of resources because we are not. ... I don't understand. It's as if we don't care.'

'This table proposed to run a budget-based Pour Tous to the FAMC [a fully funded grocery outlet, where Aurovilians could get what they needed without paying for it directly, just like the original Pour Tous "basket"], and they shot it down', Ralph continues. 'They didn't even understand. This is where Auroville is. Fifty years. ... It's a failure for me', he says, with a disappointment that pierces my spirit, or rather, the Aurovilian spirit in me. 'To commercialize [services], that would be the easy path', he adds. 'And it'll be efficient, but that's not the Auroville I want.' (Fieldnotes from BCC Meeting, 31 August 2017)

In the previous exchange, BCC members are critically assessing, and mourning, the erosion of 'pure' services, ones fully funded by the central City Services Budget to provide for Aurovilians without charging them money and key to the establishing Auroville as the economic 'real utopia' envisaged by The Mother. However, they find themselves unable to reverse this trend – the Pour Tous proposal, for instance, being rejected by their overseeing body, the FAMC, which continued to introduce policies that move away from a 'pure' services model for the sector. According to the new 2017 'Code of conduct' for unit executives (Auroville Foundation, 2017: 17), drafted by the FAMC and Working Committee, any service funding more than 50 per cent of its own running costs should contribute 33 per cent of their profits to the communal fund – just like Auroville's commercial units do. At the same time, it should be understood that the move of asking income-generating services to contribute a percentage of profits sought to address situations in which services were perceived as being such in name only, conveniently avoiding contributing to the Central Fund given their service status.

Nonetheless, administering services and commercial units in the same way further erodes the identity of the former as belonging to a space of provisioning outside of the market, even normalizing services operating at a profit – something which is antithetical to their originally conceived role and reflective of the current trend of neoliberalization. The introduction of the policy is a direct consequence of the administratively untenable 'double standard' raised in the preceding excerpted conversation, in which services are required to charge yet expected not to operate at a profit. It represents what a BCC member described as the "easy path", which unfortunately institutionalizes a further departure from Auroville's communal economic ideals – and highlights the difficulty of establishing prefigurative utopias within the constraints of the present and influence of mainstream trends, in this case, of a capitalist logic.

Maintenances: the individualized component of collective provisioning

Maintenances – individually allocated provisions – complement centrally funded services in providing for the basic needs of Aurovilians, and this section will explore how their design and implementation negotiates and reflects the challenges of institutionalizing Auroville's economic ideals. As previously highlighted, at the time of its emergence, the Maintenance system was criticized for being a standardized, individualized exchange between each community member and the collective through, at least in part, the allocation of money, which for many was – and still is – a contradiction with the founding principles of Auroville's communal economy. These attitudes still exist today, with, in addition, the complaint that the cash portion of Maintenances are too low[24] – recently exacerbated by the rising cost of living in India and the cost of increasing numbers of services being pushed to users. That said, their design does reflect Auroville's core economic ideals – a collective economy in which the basic needs of community members are centrally provided for with no exchange of money – even though it does not fully meet them. I refer here to the Full-Time City Services Maintenance, as it is the standard centrally designed, administered and disbursed adult Maintenance; there also exist a Part-Time Maintenance, Children's Maintenance, Student Maintenance and Apprentice Maintenance. Notably, Maintenances awarded to Aurovilians working in the community's commercial sector are not centrally budgeted for and administered by the BCC, as commercial units are income generating and thus have capacity to remunerate them directly. Often, these Maintenances do not follow the split portions outlined in the following but are disbursed fully in 'cash'; there is also flexibility in the amounts remunerated.

Maintenances and the ideal of 'no exchange of money'

To mitigate the exchange of money, in each account, City Services Maintenances are split in designated INR currency amounts into both 'in-kind' and 'cash' portions (see Table 6.1). While the cash credit can be withdrawn as Indian rupees and freely used by Aurovilians, either inside or outside Auroville,[25] the 'in-kind' portion cannot. Rather, it can only be transferred to and from other Auroville Financial Service accounts, so that it effectively acts like a local currency, a measure adopted worldwide to strengthen the economies of local communities (see North, 2014).

To maintain the element of collective provisioning, a portion of the standard City Services Maintenance is automatically allocated each month to a variety of services and collective funds in Auroville that provide for the basic needs of Aurovilians, notably, health and food. This is allocated

Table 6.1: Auroville Full-Time City Services Maintenances: 2007/08–2017/18

Financial year	Cash	Kind	Pour Tous	Lunch	Health	Total
2007–08	2,000	3,000	500	750	250	Rs. 6,500
2008–09	2,000	3,000	500	780	265	Rs. 6,545
2009–10	2,000	3,500	500	780	280	Rs. 7,060
2010–11	2,300	3,500	1,000	860	280	Rs. 7,940
2011–12	2,500	3,850	1,100	950	300	Rs. 8,700
2012–13	2,500	4,500	1,200	950	300	Rs. 9,450
2013–14	2,900	5,150	1,200	1,150	330	Rs. 10,730
2014–15	3,300	5,150	1,200	1,300	400	Rs. 11,350
2015–16	5,000	5,000	1,200	1,430	450	Rs. 13,080
2016–17	5,000	5,000	1,200	1,570	450	Rs. 13,220
2017–18	5,500	5,500	1,700	1,730	450	Rs. 14,880

Notes: Legend: Cash = INR amount for use within Auroville (between accounts of Auroville's Financial Service) or for withdrawal; Kind = INR amount for use exclusively within Auroville (between accounts of Auroville's Financial Service); Pour Tous = INR amount allocated to an Auroville grocery service in the name of the individual Maintenance receiver; Lunch = INR amount allocated to an Auroville community kitchen service to provide lunch for the individual Maintenance receiver on a daily basis; Health = INR amount transferred to the Auroville Health Fund to cover the cost of membership of the individual Maintenance receiver.

Source: Auroville Social Research Centre.

in the name of the individual and/or family, who can then avail of the 'in-kind' credit at the services. Aurovilians have some freedom in these allocations – for example, they can choose the eatery to which their lunch credit is transferred – and can also choose to allocate more of their in-kind credit in this way to optional services, such as Nandini, a clothing, linens and tailoring outfit.

On the basis of need: the allocation of City Services Maintenances

Maintenances are allocated to those engaging in work for the community, in principle, if an individual 'needs' it; this is informed by the founding economic ideal of economic support from the community at large being awarded to individuals on the basis of 'need' and in response to their participation in the project. The allocation of Maintenances is undertaken by the BCC Care team, a team of BCC members that disburses Maintenances as budgeted for each specific service. If someone newly joins a service and would like to be awarded a City Services Maintenance, the service manager will typically make a request of the BCC Care team, who will allocate a

Maintenance to the individual if there are any remaining in the service's approved budget (and consider allocating a Contingency Maintenance if not, usually following an in-person meeting). As previously mentioned, there are other kinds of Maintenances available – such as a Personal and Social Support Maintenance for people who are not able to work for a given reason, or an Other Auroville Activities Maintenance for individuals who work in multiple areas of community life. In such cases, the BCC Care team will typically meet the individuals to further understand their situation and financial need. Determining the latter is based on goodwill – the BCC Care team does not formally investigate whether Aurovilians have extra-Auroville assets, bank accounts or incomes. While some feel this information should be accessible, many Aurovilians are against this – in keeping with a culture of respecting the individual sphere within the collective, enacting Sri Aurobindo's (1972: 499) principle of spiritualized community, 'unity in diversity', a foundational ideal for Auroville.

Standardized City Services Maintenances: balancing individual and collective provisioning

City Services Maintenances are a standard amount, with fixed allocations of the cash and in-kind portions.[26] Aside from the concerns with Maintenances being an 'individuated' form of provision, there is also concern regarding their standardization. This is an issue because it goes against the economic ideals of Auroville, in which people participate how they feel called to and receive what they need. There is also criticism and resentment towards standardized Maintenances because these are based on a predetermination of people's 'basic needs' by Auroville's economic working groups, which some Aurovilians feel is misjudged. To my knowledge, no in-depth evaluation has been undertaken on what Aurovilians feel their needs are – certainly not recently – although this is something the FAMC did intend to undertake.[27]

Although many Aurovilians complain that the City Services Maintenance is too low, it has never been raised significantly – only in accordance with rising costs of living. In 2018, for instance, the BCC raised the Maintenance level for the first time in several years to match the rising cost of living due to the introduction of a new, comprehensive 'Goods and Services Tax' (GST) by India's central government. Increasing Maintenances is not a default measure because of the ongoing concern that these constitute an 'individuated' system of provisioning that contradicts Auroville's communal economic ideals. When I was sitting in on meetings in which raising Maintenances due to GST was discussed, several members insisted that the in-kind portion of the Maintenance would have to be increased if the cash portion were to be. If not, we would be moving towards an even more individuated and cash-based economy. If the group was considering raising Maintenances, some felt they should first consider whether existing services could be further subsidized instead, or new services created, to better provide for Aurovilians given that such measures would reduce the exchange of money in Auroville, one of the community's core economic aims. Indeed, in 2022, a community budgeting process lead by the BCC sought community input on priority sectors to fund from the communal budget (BCC, 2022).

The BCC, and other Aurovilians, are well aware that the standardized Maintenance policy is not responsive to the diversity of individual needs, with one economic administrator I interviewed maintaining that upholding a communal definition of individuals' 'basic needs' is a 'fallacy' for the Auroville project.[28] However, how to administer Maintenances in a 'subjectively objective' manner is hard to envisage institutionalizing at a community scale. In a BCC discussion centred on this, one member said:

> 'I agree that a person can have more than me *if he needs it*. I don't need Rs. 10,000, but I know people who need more than Rs. 10,000. I like the idea of having more flexibility to allocate according to needs, but it's very subjective; to implement it is very difficult.' (BCC member, 14 September 2017)[29]

Chapter 7 will explore smaller-scale, collective accounts experiments that sought to uphold such flexibility, as well as an attempt to institutionalize their organizing principles and administrative practices in an Auroville service.

Conclusion: is Auroville in a prefigurative state of bureaucratization?

Auroville's historical trajectory clearly shows that Aurovilians have intentionally and strategically developed a communal economic framework that seeks to prefigure an 'Auroville economy', though we have and continue to face financial, legal and administrative challenges in doing so, as well as competing approaches to addressing these. Interestingly, the process of establishing an alternative economic organization based on our economic ideals has included the repurposing of disruptive elements, such as Maintenances introduced to channel Indian government funding. It seems clear that Aurovilians have successfully engaged in the exercise of establishing a 'real utopia' (Wright, 2010) or 'concrete utopia' (Bloch, 1986) – both terms that Marxist scholars use to describe existing projects grounded in the material conditions of the present, while seeking to transform these. As evidenced in this chapter, community members remain self-critical of our trajectories and outcomes, demonstrating a 'critical' utopianism in an additional sense of the term, coined by Moylan (1986: 10) to convey 'critical' in the sense of both 'critical mass' and 'critique'.

In terms of outcome, perhaps most notable is that our economic organization has not yet succeeded in securing core prefigurative aspects of this economic utopia, such as providing for the basic needs of Aurovilians collectively, outside of the realm of the market. In terms of process, there are concerns around the bureaucratization of Auroville's communal administration – a predictable phase, according to Weber (Weber et al, 1978) – and its impact on a felt sense of community, even though the policies that abound do intend to capture community-level agreements based on clarity and fairness. As we have seen, the process of economic administration of the communal fund retains prefigurative characteristics of flexibility and responsiveness, something that led me to describe its nature as 'subjectively objective', as well as reflexivity demonstrated on the part of its managing team, the BCC. In response to reading a draft of this chapter, one member offered the following reflection:

> Yes, that's a real question: how is it that most of those who apply the current policies do so while regretting that this is so? Could they have led themselves into a trap? That is to say, instead of inventing new forms of management of the collective they relied on proven methods, rationally bureaucratic, quantitatively objectifying, which have their own consequences? The question is open. (Personal communication, BCC member, 25 May 2019)

Figure 6.3: Sri Aurobindo, writing

Source: Sri Aurobindo Ashram (no date[b]).

This raises the bigger question of whether the phase of bureaucratization that Auroville has entered will necessarily stifle a prefigurative process, or whether such bureaucratization could be engaged prefiguratively. In the Auroville context, this would require that it maintain a certain subjectivity in its character, in Sri Aurobindo's spiritualized sense of the term (see Figure 6.3), highlighted to me by a fellow Aurovilian: "Sri Aurobindo defines a society as 'subjective' when its individuals have found their psychic being and want to live under its influence. ... He speaks of the principles of organization of the communal life of a 'subjectivized' society – imagines systems that surpass objectivity, that draw on another dimension" (interview with 'Arthur', 29 November 2017) (see Sri Aurobindo, 1997: 246–61). Next, we turn to how Aurovilians have engaged in prefigurative, collective economic experiments outside the sphere of economic administration that are intentionally predicated on subjectivity and flexibility, and on how these have contested, informed and engaged with it in shaping the community's institutional economic development in accordance with Auroville's economic ideals.

The Institutional Potential of Prefigurative Experiments: The Evolution of Collective Accounts in Auroville

Introduction

> New forms are needed for the manifestation of a new Force.
>
> The Mother, 2003c: 90

Throughout the community's history, Aurovilians have experimented with various, alternative socio-economic forms of association that have sought to embody the community's ideals, as outlined by The Mother in her statements for how the township would be organized as an economic community and inspired by Sri Aurobindo's writings on flexible, subjective systems of collective organization. While Chapter 6 explored the development of Auroville's overarching communal economic administration, the current chapter examines economic experiments outside of this 'public sector' that ultimately informed it. The emergence and development of these experiments from the private to the public sphere is revelatory of the various levels of political agency that shape Auroville's economic practices and organization – including activist community members, community administrators and government advisors – which is significant in understanding the anarchic and 'transgressive' (Sargisson, 2000: 1) nature of its utopian practice.

We will focus on the evolution of a series of experiments in common accounts and how these prefigured unique cooperative public services in the community, delving into a case study of one such service – the PTDC – to explore the process of its establishment and ongoing challenges in its development. The latter will continue to be revelatory of how Aurovilians engage in a critical prefigurative practice and how this dimension of critique can both fuel and stall its progress. Such insight into the unique model and experience of Auroville's cooperatives will hopefully serve the development of the already wide-ranging practice of cooperative economic practices and organizations worldwide.

Common accounts in Auroville

I discovered the practice of common accounts in Auroville at Sunday lunch at home with my parents. Like in virtually every conversation at a family meal, we had wound up talking about Auroville – a habit that preceded my research, though the latter fomented it. On this particular Sunday, I had expressed concern over economic inequality in our community and was raising questions about how Aurovilians who struggled financially were, or could be, supported economically.

"Well, we had the Common Account", ventured my mother, Nicole. I had never heard of it. "Who started that?", I first asked. "We did!", she answered. "Who's 'we'?", I retorted, thinking she meant Auroville at large. Nicole pointed at herself, while saying "and Peter", my dad. I was taken aback, as I had been many times throughout the course of my research, in discovering ways in which they had been involved in Auroville historically. "I was in the Financial Service at the time", Nicole explained; "I created the Common Account, and managed it, from there." I asked her how many people were members, expecting it to be a low number, like 12. My parents answered at the same time: "100", said Nicole; "50", said Peter. "What did you say?", Peter asked Nicole, in a tone of incredulous disbelief; "200?", "100", she replied, self-assuredly. "I think it was more like 70", he countered. "80", she said, conceding but clearly unconvinced.

Nicole explained that they all put money into the Common Account at the beginning of the month and used the Common Account for their everyday expenses. Individual usage was tracked, though this seemed to be primarily so that people who "had money" would give 10 per cent extra on what they had used the previous month, so as to even out the balance for those who "didn't have money". People who were struggling financially could also come forward to the groups with specific funding requests – an example she gave was an electrical moped – and the group would see if they could support it. I asked my parents whether the Common Account was a successful experiment, and Nicole responded, "Well, we were careful not to include anybody who was known to be financially irresponsible." When starting out, they had approached people they knew, who they thought would be interested. Once established, how did they decide if someone new could join? Nicole could not remember.

When I asked my parents who were members of the Common Account, I discovered it was not the only sharing account of its kind. Nicole started listing some names – "Françoise … Alain Bernard …" – when Peter interrupted her. "Alain Bernard?", he questioned, "I thought he was in Seed." I'd never heard of Seed either and said as much. "Well people *still* don't know it exists!", Nicole remarked. "It still exists?", I exclaimed, even more surprised. "Yes", said Nicole, "Otto [a current executive of the Financial Service] manages it."

"Does the Common Account still exist?", I asked, now wondering if my parents had been part of some shared account I did not know about for all these years. "No, no", said Nicole, "it dwindled after we left [Auroville, for family reasons, to France for four years]. We started it in the early 1990s." All of sudden it clicked. I knew that the 1990s had been a time of contested change to Auroville's economic organization, following the adoption of the individualized 'Maintenance' system triggered by Auroville's economic relationship with the Ministry of Education of the central Indian government (recounted in Chapter 6). "Was it in reaction to the creation of individual accounts that was happening around that time?", I remarked. "Yes, yes!", said Nicole, emphatically.

I met with Otto in the Financial Service shortly afterwards to talk about Seed. He told me it was also started in the wake of the creation of the Financial Service in the early 1990s by a small group who "wanted to do something different, wanted something collective – not an individuated system".[1] We notice here the same impetus, that is, disappointment with a shift away from the collective ethos underpinning the community's economic ideals, galvanized into prefigurative action that reclaimed this. As we will see, the founding ideals around work in Auroville – that everyone in the community would contribute to it through work, but that this would be a practice of spiritual development and not a way to earn a living, with Aurovilians' livelihood needs secured collectively – were crucial in informing the raison d'être of this common account. Moreover, the ideal of 'unity in diversity' (Sri Aurobindo, 1972: 499), which strongly informs how Auroville envisions itself as a community, was key to how it was managed.

When Seed was started, there was only one formal requirement for people to join – that the person worked full-time in Auroville – while perceived adherence to the community's economic ideals, as outlined, were critical in securing membership. Just like with the Common Account, the small group who came up with the idea for Seed approached others who they knew might be interested in doing something different. The vast majority of members (30) had been there from the very beginning of the fund, and no one had joined in recent years. Otto said it was not promoted, in part, because 30 was a manageable size and, in part, because the most important thing was trust – a trust that the existing members had now built over 30 years. For it to work, Otto said it was key that there was "affinity" between people, which I came to understand meant an affinity in terms of their commitment to Auroville's economic ideals.[2]

Members with no individual savings sometimes required capital beyond the monthly subsistence amounts that they contributed into the account, and when I asked for what kind of expenses, Otto's response was revelatory of how much the existence of the fund was underpinned by Auroville's founding economic ideals:

'Flight tickets, or maybe something for the house, that may not be covered by Housing [the Housing Service, whose Fraternity Fund funded or subsidized repairs]. The issue is that we know a Maintenance doesn't cover all the basic needs, and then people are doing extra work for money and neglect what they should do, which is exactly what we didn't want to have happening here [in Auroville], where work is supposed to be a help in one's own development.' (Interview with Otto, member of Seed, 26 October 2017)

However, people who had asked to join in more recent years on the basis of being financially strained were not admitted. While the fund did function in a solidary way, including members whose only source of income was the Auroville Maintenance – an amount insufficient for many in meeting their costs of living – charity was not reason enough to accept someone. Those driven primarily by financial self-interest were not perceived as sharing the same collective ethos that bound the group; solidarity with the latter stemmed from a shared sense of commitment to prefiguring the socio-economic ideals of Auroville and a trust that had been built up over time.

The administration of the fund was also prefigurative of the flexible, subjective systems that Sri Aurobindo had described for a spiritualized society (see Sri Aurobindo, 1997) and the ideal of 'unity and diversity' (Sri Aurobindo, 1972: 499) that Auroville aspired to embody in its articulations of community – in this case, economic. The account functioned similarly to the Common Account: everybody transferred in their Maintenance, or more if they had private funds and could afford to, though this was not imposed; they all used individual accounts for their everyday charges; and at the end of each month, Seed would cover the expenses of each. Pluses and minuses on individual expenditures relative to their contributions were absorbed by the common account, which had an administrator who kept track of these and addressed any issues if necessary.

I decided to meet 'Arthur',[3] Seed's administrator, to find out more about how this worked. "Each person could administer a common account in their own way", he started by saying. We were in the library, where Arthur also worked. "Personally, I don't take any risks; I continue to track on an individual basis", he said, a statement that perhaps betrayed the desirability of not doing so given the community's ideals around collectivism. He only informs individuals, however, if there are major discrepancies between their expenditures and contributions. "If they have a big positive balance, I inform them – when people don't have ample means, I inform them if it's positive", Arthur explained to me:

> 'Same thing for the negative. I don't tell them they have to reimburse it; I simply inform them. If it continues, I go and meet them to find out if it's due to financial issues. I ask them to reimburse the fund *if* they can. If they can't, I put their balance back to zero.'

Not requiring individuals to meet expenditures they were unable to, even if they had personally incurred them, is revelatory of how the ethos of the fund was informed by the ideal of a collective responsibility of care in Auroville for members of the community – something that Arthur underscored in saying: "In the Aurovilian community, if you have an economic problem, it is not *your* problem. It is a problem for the community to take responsibility for" (interview with Arthur, administrator of Seed, 29 November 2017). Managing the fund in a way that was responsive to the unique situations of individuals, rather than by arbitrary rules, is demonstrative of the aforementioned 'subjective objectivity' that is threaded through much of Auroville's administrative practice – inspired by The Mother's anarchic statements that there would be no fixed rules framed for the community (The Mother, 2003a: 261, 266) and that a diversity of individual expressions would be upheld within it, following Sri Aurobindo's (1972: 499) principle of 'unity in diversity'.

Seed's financial health allowed for this flexible administration because, over the years, a considerable credit had built up from unused monthly budgets and from additional funds people would deposit into it. "The collective *generates* money", Arthur affirmed; "No one is left in need, it covers the needs of those who would not be able to do so individually *and* it builds up credit." This credit was so significant that a savings account, '*Sangha*' ('community' in Sanskrit), had been created alongside the Seed current account. In addition to subsidizing the regular living expenses of some, the savings of Seed were used to fund 'special needs' of members and even to grant significant interest-free loans to Auroville projects and services that members were involved in.

This is especially significant to note in connection with Elinor Ostrom's (1990) work on reclaiming the commons, which demonstrates that communal resources can be successfully managed and not fall prone to the free-rider effect, contrary to what the 'tragedy of the commons' theory suggests (Hardin, 1968). Among the principles she defines as key for their effective maintenance are clear boundaries, such as membership, and clear monitoring, such as the tracking of expenditures, both of which were assured in the case of Seed.

Interestingly, Otto told me that he had tried at one point to strengthen this savings account by suggesting that people pool all of their money into it but that it had not worked. Clearly, individuals only felt comfortable experimenting with a part of their individual wealth in this communal exercise, something that reflects an overarching trend in Auroville: many members, both Indian and non-Indian, keep a significant portion of their wealth in bank accounts or assets outside of the community. Some feel we should all invest individual financial assets into our community accounts in solidary support of our economy; however, most who have the possibility prefer to ensure their continued financial independence from the community by investing significant amounts outside of it.

This capacity to define one's balance between individuality and community I consider to be one key to the overall success of the Auroville community in terms of longevity in light of the scholarship on intentional community that identifies the curtailing of individual freedoms as detrimental for members in the long term, sometimes leading to the collapse of communities (Kanter, 1972). Interestingly, when I asked whether there were any guidelines regarding what people could spend money on, Otto said, "No, because people have different needs", adding: "Ashram 'needs' are not the same 'needs', but we don't want to be like the Ashram." This last statement underscores how Aurovilians embody the ideal of 'unity in diversity' (Sri Aurobindo, 1972: 499) of affirming individual freedom within the framework of community and how important this is in distinguishing themselves from other types of intentional communities that insist on commonality, achieved through adherence to universal rules.

Circles: a first attempt at scaling the practice of common accounts

The success of Seed drew the attention of the chair of the Auroville Foundation, the legal entity that was created to formally recognize the community under India's Ministry of Education. Kireet Joshi suggested that the Seed experiment be scaled up through multiplication in the community. This recommendation coincided with a feeling within the community of being "off-track with our collective economy",[4] one that was resurgent during my fieldwork period. A series of community-wide meetings ensued, in which Aurovilians explored the possibility of creating several common accounts, which were called 'Circles'.

The Circles experiment started out "full of people, idealism, enthusiasm",[5] but despite the fact that this top-down suggestion was embraced within the community, it failed to successfully take root. Otto said that it was because "it doesn't work with people who have nothing to do with each other".[6] He told me that most Circles fell apart in six months to a year, while some of them never even started because they got stuck in endless discussions, trying to agree on the conditions for their Circle. "For it to work, there has to be trust", Otto emphasized, adding that the Seed group hardly ever meets because "it's not needed – we've known each other for 30 years".[7]

One Circle – 'Maheswari' – does still exist today. Just like Seed, it has no rules about personal expenditures, except for one: that members purchase and consume at Auroville enterprises "because the whole thing was about supporting the collective economy".[8] However, 'Rebecca'[9] remarked "it was not a rule but an understanding. We were close-knit." Trust and affinity were thus key for the success and longevity of both Seed and Maheswari. Unlike Seed, Maheswari did not even track individual expenditures – Rebecca said she felt it was antithetical to the idea of a common pot. Only when the account went into minus did they check in order to understand why.

Since members trust each other, they do not worry that money is being misspent. However, this was not always the case. When they started out, the expenditures of some of the members were unacceptable to the group at large. One example was the purchase of a car (a luxury item in India), another was the use of the common account to finance a large loan on new property. While the members were never formally expelled from the Circle, there were numerous "heated and emotional discussions" related to their spending, and they eventually left the group.[10]

More than one Circle faced the issue of significant differences in how members related to the accounts – some with "aspirations for free money",[11] while others "very idealistically gave everything they had".[12] Arthur, the administrator of Seed, considered the Circles experiment flawed because these common accounts were perceived by many as a way to increase their purchasing power, rather than as tools for the development of individual and collective consciousness.

'Siobhan',[13] a member of the 'New Dawn' Circle, felt that many of those who did approach these idealistically were "let down" and that this happened "too many times". According to her account, New Dawn Circle had worked very well for two to three years until it "ended with a crash!" when one member bankrupted the common pot. He decided to leave the community, purchasing expensive clothes and shoes before doing so, and leaving his teenage daughter behind for the group to support financially.[14]

She nonetheless considers the Circle to have been a useful experiment because it was a "lively process of people coming together for interesting discussions and ideas for an internal and in-kind economy for Auroville". a collective learning process that, as we shall see, was prefigurative of a successfully institutionalized communal accounting system, the basis of the community provisioning service: the Pour Tous Distribution Centre

(PTDC). She also emphasized the learning aspect of the New Dawn Circle at an individual level, relating it to the prefigurative process of becoming Aurovilian; she highlighted how participating in such an experiment required Aurovilians to "lose the sense of personal possession" – a line from The Mother's (1971) text *To Be a True Aurovilian*. This required a change of consciousness, Siobhan remarked, thus pinning the potential of such an experiment to succeed on the evolution of spiritual consciousness that Integral Yoga was predicated upon. Unfortunately, New Dawn failed to safeguard itself from the lack of consciousness of just one of its members and thus failed as a discrete common account – a high price to pay for a group experiment. How effective a tool it was for members to develop that change of consciousness, however, would be difficult to ascertain.

Prosperity: connecting common accounts experiments with social services

In 2006, after the collapse of the Circles experiment, a group of Aurovilians set up the shared savings account 'Prosperity' and concurrently established the PTDC, the cooperative grocery that we will explore next. Members of Prosperity contribute a small, standard monthly amount into the fund,[15] from which they can seek financial support in times of need for expenditures incurred at designated Auroville services that provide for 'basic needs', thus beginning to explore a collectively organized provision for basic needs.[16] These included the PTDC cooperative grocery, a clothing and linens service named 'Nandini' and the Auroville Dental Service (as this is not included in the Health Fund, which all Aurovilians are encouraged to be members of), as well as, previously, Auroville's central community kitchen (the Solar Kitchen), before lunch became a centrally funded 'in-kind' provision within City Services Maintenances.

My conversation with its administrator, Arthur (the same person who managed the common account Seed), revealed once again a resistance to bureaucratization. I was trying to understand how Prosperity worked in practice and asked whether people came to him with bills from one or more of the services to be paid out of the fund. Arthur virtually bounded, responding in volley: "I don't need the bill. Sometimes, people offer it to me, but I don't want it. The idea is not to check – it's not an insurance. That's not the idea at all" (interview with Arthur, administrator of Prosperity, 29 November 2017). If members had to be policed, the project was pointless as an experiment in prefiguring a spiritualized society, which, as Arthur shared with me, Sri Aurobindo (2014: 21–3) had envisaged would develop 'subjective'[17] forms of communal organization. Instead of being based on objective and uniformly imposed rules, these would be responsive to the spiritual evolution of individuals and thus able to foster the spiritual evolution of a collective (Sri Aurobindo, 1997): "Prosperity for everyone, there's no point in creating it because it already exists [in the world] – with policies, which are detestable but indispensable. administrators become cops – there is no point in that."[18] He explained that such 'subjective' experiments could not be "forced" into being; rather, they had to correspond with the perceptions and experiences of those participating within them. For this reason, just like Seed, Prosperity is not advertised. For a decade, the fund covered all member requests without running into financial issues, with no policy for how much any individual could 'claim'. In 2017, the fund collapsed, and Arthur asks himself why this happened: "Because the prices have increased?[19] Because people consumed more?" His questions sound both genuine and rhetorical at the same time. "I think maybe people started using it as an insurance", he said – by which I assume he meant taking advantage of an opportunity to be refunded, rather than reserving this for times of need. "The downside is that few people participate in these kinds of collective economic experiments, because they are not interested", he remarked, as our conversation drew to a close; "That's my assumption; you'll be able to tell me what you've found at the end of your research." I tried to say that I was not even aware of them and that perhaps communicating such experiments would draw more people in. Arthur brushed this off, saying it was up to people who were interested to be drawn to finding out about them.[20]

What I have noticed is that those who were not early community members are, overwhelmingly, unfamiliar with the history of Auroville, including that of its economic development. Many Aurovilians are critical of the shortcomings of our present economic organization(s) in terms of embedding Auroville's socio-economic ideals, some with little awareness of the experiments attempted and challenges faced in arriving at the present stage. In revealing the latter, I hope not only that more understanding will be achieved but also that it will empower people to take this collective prefigurative process forward, without 'reinventing the wheel', as is often pointed out.

As the history of Auroville's common accounts shows, these were instigated by community members as a means to contest the individuation of economic support triggered by a government funding interface, for they perceived this to be a critical breach from the existing communal economic organization of the community and from its socio-economic ideals. Common accounts allowed a funnelling of individual, government-funded stipends into collectively administered funds by Aurovilians, thereby constituting an opportunity to actively reclaim and enact their ideals. As such, Aurovilians exercised both what Moylan (1986: 10) theorizes as 'critical' utopianism by challenging developments within their own community and what Sargisson (2000: 1) terms a 'transgressive' utopianism in developing alternative practices that politicized personal spheres to effect change in the public sphere. Although many of these common accounts failed, they were instrumental in prefiguring the community's existing cooperative institutions, a case study of which we turn to now.

The Pour Tous Distribution Center

Just like the first common accounts, the PTDC emerged in protest to a socio-economic trajectory that was perceived as antithetical to Auroville's collective ideals. In the early 2000s, funding for a new facility for Pour Tous (the historical provisioning service for members of the community described in Chapter 6) prompted a group of about ten concerned individuals – including my mother – to gather and reflect on how this new outlet could be run in a way that would reaffirm Auroville's evolution towards the communal economy envisaged by The Mother, in which Aurovilians would give what they could in terms of work and involvement, and have their basic needs met without the exchange of money, through centrally supported services.

They felt compelled to do so because the existing institution, which had started out as a solidary common pot, had devolved into what they perceived to be an ordinary, profit-making shop, something they felt deeply disappointed by: "Thirty years to arrive to the point where we were just selling and buying to each other!",[21] one of the members exclaimed to me. While the existing Pour Tous was located in the current outskirts of the community,[22] the new site was centrally located in the Service Area: a complex of services that included the community kitchen (Solar Kitchen), the Nandini clothing and linens service, the Free Store (where community members brought clothing items they no longer used and could pick up anything they wished for free) and ServiceLink, the central administrative hub of services.

The PTDC group – composed of several members of the Auroville Board of Services – felt that the existing Pour Tous model would be incongruent with the ethos of these other services, in addition to being incongruent with the socio-economic ideals of Auroville in general, and feared that:

> '[I]f we were not going to run this outlet as a community service without the exchange of money, because it was at the centre of Auroville, we could say goodbye to Auroville as a society without the exchange of money, where people are supported, they give what they can in terms of work and involvement, and they receive what they need without exchange on money, which is what it's supposed to be.' (Interview with Nicole, PTDC Support Group member, 12 April 2016)

At the time, Pour Tous, despite being registered as a 'self-supporting service' – a solidary organization meant to provide for everyday needs of the community, levying only enough to cover its cost of operation and development – was in fact generating a substantial profit. This was a significant breach of ethics because its profit was being derived from charging Aurovilians a mark-up for basic needs, which should be provided for with no exchange of money according to the community's ideals. At the time of my doctoral research, a review and reform of the service, renamed the 'Pour Tous Purchasing Centre', was being undertaken by the community's key economic groups, the BCC and the FAMC, and by 2021, a new management team had been put in place and budgetary support was under way.

The PTDC group sought to elaborate guidelines that would more closely reflect the community's socio-economic ideals. In brief, the concept was that the PTDC would operate as a cooperative, in which members would contribute a certain amount monthly and then take whatever they felt amounted to their 'basic needs'. The service would be centrally supported, not self-supporting, meaning that the operating costs, such as the overhead expenses and the Maintenances of Aurovilians working in the service, would be borne by the collective through the Central Fund administered by the BCC. The group presented the concept to the BCC in 2005, with 160 people ready to participate in the experiment.[23]

The request was strongly challenged by the BCC[24] for a number of reasons. One was the concern that fully supported services were too much of a drain on the collective economy – self-supporting services were preferable.[25] Another was that the PTDC model, which was based on membership, did not warrant collective funds.[26] Furthermore, it was anticipated that the model of participation would be abused: people would take more than they contributed; the service would end up financially overdrawn; and the Central Fund would be compelled to bear the cost.[27]

After many difficult meetings, the Economy Group (eventually renamed the 'Budget Coordination Committee' [BCC]) decided to award the new Pour Tous a small budget – Rs. 38,000 monthly – and a time for experimentation.[28] The service began to operate in 2006, with many involved in running it doing so on a voluntary basis,[29] and membership more than doubled in the first year (Thomas and Thomas, 2013: 102). At the end of the first year, in 2007, the Economy Group (BCC) called for a general meeting[30] to determine whether the experiment should continue to run and be supported by the Central Fund.[31] According to the group active in launching the PTDC, the Economy Group was "certain" the outcome of the meeting would be to end the PTDC experiment and that was their motive for calling it.[32] However, the community at large ended up resonating with the PTDC project:

> 'What works in Auroville is when you have actually a small group of people who are cognizant of what they are doing and who really try to

work it out in detail and come to the community with something that makes sense and that's congruent with what Auroville is supposed to be, is understanding of the possibilities and limitations of today, and is able to come up with a project that can stand. And if you do that, you have people behind you ... because you still have a majority of people in Auroville who really come for these ideals. So, when something happens like that, there is a resonance. There was a resonance in that meeting. It was like, "Yeah, this is what we want."' (Interview with Nicole, PTDC Support Group member, 12 April 2016)

Since 2007, budgetary support and community participation in the PTDC has increased. Its running costs – the stipends of Aurovilians working in the service, the transport of goods and the maintenance costs of the building that houses the service – are fully subsidized by Auroville's communal budget,[33] while the goods it carries are purchased with fixed monthly contributions by the cooperative's members. Contributions from participants are collected into a single common account and used to procure a range of items that correspond primarily to the category of 'basic needs' (vegetarian food products, such as grains, lentils, fruits and vegetables, and household items, such as personal care and cleaning supplies), alongside other certain criteria, such as affordability, healthiness, quality and eco-friendliness. Auroville products are prioritized, and several Auroville commercial units offer their products at a cost price or on a discounted basis. The 'spirit of service' is a key criterion for the acceptance of items proposed by Auroville units or Aurovilian home-made products; the PTDC avoids carrying goods whose price is inflated in order to derive profit on purchase, as this goes against the ideals of service and fraternity that were at the core of the cooperative (see Figure 7.1).[34]

The physical space was intentionally designed with all shelving along the walls and a largely free and empty space in the middle, consciously avoiding conventional supermarket rows that do not invite people to pause or interact comfortably with others, to create instead an informal community meeting space (see Figure 7.2). Interaction between participants is the norm, many greeting one another with affection and entering into conversation, ranging from personal matters to those of concern in community life and functioning.

Its membership in 2018 was 1,500 people, which represents the majority of the Auroville population, and there was a waiting list of individuals who would like to join. The PTDC is open to Aurovilians, Newcomers and long-term volunteers, though lack of human resources and an intricate accounting system make it challenging to continue to scale and are in the process of being addressed. The service refers to its members as 'participants' in order to emphasize that this is a participatory, collective experiment – language that is drawn from a statement The Mother (2003a: 261) made about Auroville: 'All who live there will participate in its life and development.'

Figure 7.1: The PTDC

Monthly contributions

Each participant pays a monthly contribution based on an estimate of the consumption patterns of their household. This amount is collected into a single common account used by the PTDC cooperative to purchase the products. The running costs are covered by Auroville's communal budget.

Conscious consumption

Participants of the PTDC cooperative can take as many products as they feel they need. A balance sheet is kept and participants are called to align their monthly contribution to their consumption patterns if needed.

Solidary suppliers

Many products are purchased at cost-price or discounted rates from Auroville's commercial units or farms, and from regional partners who share a similar ethos to PTDC and Auroville at large.

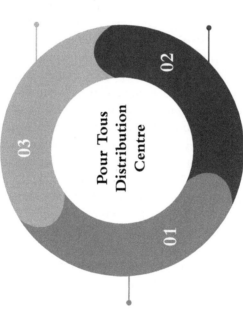

Source: Clarence-Smith and Monticelli/Springer Nature (2022).

Figure 7.2: The PTDC at lunchtime, an opportunity to interact with other community members

Source: Marco Saroldi (Auroville Digital Archives).

As per the PTDC's original guidelines, participants chose from one of three standard monthly contributions[35] as approximated their needs, but in current practice, these contribution amounts are flexible. Individuals may select any of the items available in the cooperative, and the PTDC offers a small range of items per category in an attempt to strike a balance between meeting people's needs without imposing uniformity and not encouraging a 'consumer society'.[36] This harks back to Auroville's ideal of collectivity, based on Sri Aurobindo's (1972: 499) conception of 'unity in diversity' and The Mother's (2003a: 261) statement that the community is responsible to provide for its members 'on the basis of minimum needs'. While being a 'common fund' as Pour Tous originally was, it is far more flexible in how it meets the needs of individuals, who can choose whatever they would like to take, instead of receiving a standard basket of provisions. Members are expected to contribute in relationship to their usage, which is posted on the 16th, 26th and last day of each month on the public noticeboard at the entrance of the cooperative. Usage represents the tally of the Rs. cost of the items selected by the participant to date,[37] which is tracked at a checkout counter (see Figure 7.3), though no itemized statements are provided.

The INR cost of items is not displayed on the shelves because the service would like people to focus on their needs, without their perception of these being influenced by the price of items, in addition to emphasizing that none of the items are for sale – an important ideological point the service wishes

Figure 7.3: The PTDC checkout counter (2016)

Source: Marco Saroldi (Auroville Digital Archives).

to make given The Mother's (2003a: 263) statement that there ought to be no 'internal exchange of money' in Auroville. One of the original criteria for the selection of items available at the PTDC is affordability, so that individuals subsisting on the modest Auroville Maintenance would be able to provide for their daily life while remaining within their PTDC contribution budget. However, in recent years, more expensive, high-quality products have been appearing on the shelves – such as artisanal ricotta and ice cream – bringing a consideration of price into the choice of items for some. A binder with the pricing list for all PTDC items is available for people to consult within the cooperative, but many are unaware of it; some ask the Aurovilians working at cashiers for the price of individual items.

Those participants who find themselves overdrawn can request to assess their itemized consumption costs with the PTDC managers to address this. Participants who regularly overuse are contacted throughout the year and requested to refund the service. Certain people with scarce financial means try to avoid raising their monthly contribution even if their consumption often overshoots it, preferring to pay back the service the exact amount it owes in the hopes of saving money. The service, however, tries to discourage this pattern, both because it goes against the PTDC's collective economic ethos and because it makes for more complex accounting. When collective usage is higher than collective contributions, the service also appeals to all participants to make an additional donation, if they can afford to, so that these excesses can be collectively subsidized. There are participants who intentionally choose to make monthly contributions that are higher than their relative consumption because they know that this will subsidize those that are struggling financially and feel positively when their monthly contribution exceeds their use: "I couldn't care less at the end of the month when my balance is positive that it goes to the common pot; I find that fantastic. ... It's no longer me or you; we are one. We are one. It's the collective" (interview with Ann, 16 May 2016).

The PTDC has only had to ask a handful of participants to leave the service in its decade-plus history (Auroville Radio, 2018). In one PTDC support group[38] meeting I attended, the topic of termination of membership was raised. The manager hesitantly asked about the group's view on a few individuals who were consistently overusing and failing to reimburse the service, quickly adding: "I don't like termination. Do we give them more time?" Apparently, the group had already raised this issue with these participants several times, to no avail, pointing out that if the reasons were financial difficulty, they had figured out how to help with that in the past. They decided to give those individuals a few months' notice before ending their membership and to invite them to reapply after six months. The same meeting had also been called to discuss the case of a PTDC participant who had requested to be refunded Rs. 8,000 worth of unused contribution the previous year, something that had never happened before and shocked the team for its breach of understanding of the principles of the service.

Later, I remarked to my mother, one of the founders of the service, that there seemed to be quite a few members of the PTDC who were interested in it not as a socio-economic experiment but because it was cheap and centrally located.[39] "Yes", said Nicole; "When Jocelyn and I first started PTDC, it was very important to us that only people who were in it for the socio-economic experiment aspect become members. But others believed in strength in numbers – it's one of the ways to measure success."[40] Unlike Seed and other common accounts experiments that could select members, as a public service, the PTDC is a 'mass' common account project. In light of the dissatisfaction of some with the pooling of resources aspect of the PTDC, however, the team is considering whether an eventual second location should operate as a standard capitalist shop, with individual purchasing, while nonetheless retaining its non-profit nature. In the existing PTDC, only those members who are explicitly interested in the shared account experiment would remain, which the team hopes would enable them to develop it further together.

To what extent is the PTDC prefigurative in the Auroville context?

To what extent is the PTDC 'prefigurative' of Auroville's socio-economic ideals? Opinions differ among its participants. Some feel that it represents a significant step towards the future of the Auroville economy in terms of the realization of its ideals,[41] whereas others challenge its economic model as a step towards a collective economy with no exchange of money. Uma, a member of one of Auroville's economic think tanks – the 'Economy Action Group' – felt that in successfully institutionalizing the previous rounds of experimentation around shared accounts, the PTDC has "managed to make a certain entry into that new economy and held it, and make it work and make it really work – it has crossed over this survival crunch … it has landed in the consciousness of people" (interview with Uma, PTDC participant, 5 May 2016). Ann, who had managed Pour Tous from 1983 to 1990 during its phase of transition from a collective to an individual basis of provisioning (highlighted in Chapter 6), considered the PTDC to be "the future of the Auroville economy":

'In any case of what I call the "base economy" – food, education, health … and I think PTDC will one day cover all this, and perhaps even go further. I don't yet have the vision of that, I am not an economist. But for me, it is obvious that PTDC is that … something that brings us together, that unifies us.' (Interview with Ann, PTDC participant, 16 May 2016)

Others, however, fail to see how the economic model of the PTDC is prefigurative of an economy with 'no exchange of money', in which people's needs are assured for by the collective. Each person contributes in money, and their consumption is individually tracked on the basis of the INR cost of the items they select. They are expected to contribute more if their individual expenditure does not meet their budget, and thus they consider the experiment to be flawed, even hypocritical.[42]

Many people, however, once they established what their monthly budget was on average, no longer worried about their consumption. They enjoy not having prices foregrounded and do not track their expenditure. According to Arthur, most members of Seed also have no idea what their current 'balance' in the common account is at any given time – what they know is that he is taking care of monitoring it for them, in relation to the balance of the account as a whole, and feel that "letting go is beautiful".[43]

While some PTDC participants would find it preferable to not have any individual tracking whatsoever because they consider it antithetical to the idea of a collective economy, others consider that having the PTDC take care of monitoring expenditure on their behalf is actually a step towards a communally organized economy[44] and that being reminded of the limits of their budget "is necessary at this stage of our consciousness, as very few of us may claim that they will take only what they absolutely need!"[45]

Anandi, the PTDC manager, recognizes that asking people to base their choice on need and not on prices is challenging for many at a psychological level: "How much do you take when you don't need to look at prices? What is it that you need? How do you react when you are confronted with that shelf which doesn't say any price?"[46] She points out that when people begin their membership and she asks them what their monthly budget is, most do not know, even though they have been shopping at outlets with prices up to then. To her, that is an indication that pricing each item does not actually amount to one being conscious of one's expenditure, despite some participants' exhortations to the contrary. Rather than limiting their capacity to be conscious, some participants argue that:

> 'It forces us – this is the part that interests me the most, it forces us to be conscious about what we are doing. ... There are people who complain afterwards, saying, "How come you don't show the prices?" It is up to us to be conscious. And why do I like this PTDC – it's that. It's an adventure, also of consciousness.' (Interview with Ann, PTDC participant, 16 May 2016)

In this way, the PTDC is also about unlearning old patterns and relearning new ones, which, as Siobhan had highlighted in the New Dawn Circle experiment, is key to the project of Aurovilians becoming more 'conscious'. That said, members who are financially stressed do not have as much economic and psychological freedom to experiment with doing so in practice, even if they align with the ideals in principle.

Prefiguring institutional economic relationships

A key dynamic that has been noted by those involved in the cooperative movement is how much solidarity is generated between cooperatives and that this prefigures alternative socio-economic relationships that are not predicated on profiteering from competitiveness (Antiuniversity Now, 2017). One important aspect to consider in the PTDC experiment is that it fosters relationships with Auroville's commercial units that prefigure Auroville's ideals for its economic organization. It has also formed solidary relationships with non-Aurovilian suppliers whose ethos resonate with that of the PTDC and of the Auroville community at large, and who sell their goods to the PTDC at a discounted rate.

Several of Auroville's commercial units contribute their products to the service at cost price because it operates on a zero-profit basis and caters exclusively to community members. The executives of Maroma, the highest-contributing commercial unit to the community since it was founded in the 1970s, highlight the PTDC's unique role and potential in Auroville's communal economy thanks to this model, noting that the PTDC has offered them a channel through which they can contribute their products

Figure 7.4: MG Ecoduties at the PTDC (2016)

Source: Marco Saroldi (Auroville Digital Archives).

to the community at cost price, where no other such platforms exist.[47] Margarita, an executive of MG Ecoduties, an Auroville unit that develops environmentally friendly soaps and household detergents, and supplies these at cost to the PTDC (see Figure 7.4), says that she does so because she strongly believes in a gift economy for Auroville and the PTDC is creating a paradigm shift in this regard, as it is a model based on values of the gift economy and not on a capitalistic system.[48] These and other executives with profitable businesses expressed that they foresaw donating their products to the PTDC in the future.

In this way, the PTDC prepares for what could eventually become a service that not only does not sell products to Aurovilians but also does not buy them from Auroville units, thereby realizing the community's economic ideal of operating with 'no exchange of money'. One could envisage that commercial units that would not be able to donate their products in addition to their financial contribution to the Central Fund would account for these as 'in-kind' community contributions, a mechanism that already exists for other communal provisions.

Although, as one unit executive pointed out, only few commercial units produce basic goods items that would be of use to the community, others could contribute in cash towards the purchase of such items that may be lacking. It bears noting that in its infancy, Pour Tous set the precedent for the practice of units contributing towards the collective; Claire Fanning had reached an agreement with all Auroville units that they could contribute a certain percentage to it directly (Fanning, 2011). It also aligns with The Mother's directive for the participation of industries in Auroville:

> The industries will participate actively, they will contribute. If they are industries providing articles that aren't in constant need – and are therefore in amounts or numbers too great for the township's own use, so that they will be sold outside – those industries must naturally participate through money. And I take the example of food: those who produce food will give the township what it needs (in proportion to what they produce, of course) and it is the township's responsibility to feed everyone. (The Mother, 1977: 24)

This could form part of an evolution away from an individual and towards a communal responsibility for the provision of the basic needs of community members, as she intended. The PTDC management hopes to support such a trend, envisaging that the Central Fund could allocate a 'basic needs' contribution for community members at the cooperative now that a collective budget has been ascertained through the use of one account for the purchase of goods.[49] This is already being partially prefigured by some participants having their PTDC contribution allocated to the cooperative from the cash and/or in-kind portion of their Maintenance before the latter is disbursed to their individual accounts.

Conclusion: approximating a spiritualized society

The series of common accounts experiments, leading up to and including the PTDC, have clearly been sites of prefigurative utopian practice in which Aurovilians have attempted to concretize the community's founding socio-economic ideals – such as providing for Aurovilians' basic needs collectively and eliminating the exchange of money between Aurovilians. These initiatives were driven by community members who, disappointed with the status quo of Auroville's collective economy, sought to reclaim the community's socio-economic development, thus enacting a 'critical' prefigurative utopianism (Moylan, 1986: 10).

While I have focused on the example of the PTDC in the second section of this chapter – because of how dynamic and contested an experiment it is, and the critical mass of people that participate in it – there are many other services, and other institutionalized experiments, that similarly base themselves on concretizing Auroville's socio-economic ideals. As previously mentioned, in the same Service Area that houses the PTDC, there is a clothing, linens and tailoring service, 'Nandini', founded in 1994. Just like the PTDC, its operational costs are subsidized by the Central Fund, it

Figure 7.5: Celebrating community services: the PTDC and Free Store 'Fashion Show' (2018)

Source: Marco Saroldi (Auroville Digital Archives).

undertakes bulk purchasing with member contributions, individuals take what they need and their consumption is tracked.

Another example is the Free Store, situated in between the PTDC and Nandini – a centre for donated items that is open for all Aurovilians and Newcomers to take whatever they wish to, free of cost, as the service's costs of operation are financed by the Central Fund (see Figure 7.5). Furthermore, in two recent Aurovilian housing projects, Citadines and Sunship, approximately half of the apartments are allocated for free to people with no means, their cost absorbed by premium contributions made by individuals to inhabit the other half, successfully implementing fraternal models for wealth sharing to provide for the basic need of shelter.

Citizens throughout the world who have participated in 'the provision of general interest services not provided by either the market or the government' by setting up cooperative community institutions have been theorized as enacting an 'active citizenship' (Mori, 2014: 346). In the context of Auroville, I consider this activism to be prefiguratively utopian, as community members are engaged in intentionally shaping their society, both in the present and for the future, according to the community's socio-economic ideals.

The associations that have developed in this process have evolved from private to public sphere projects, increasing in scale and institutionalization. As such, they affirm the political potential of enacting what Sargisson (2000: 1) terms a 'transgressive' utopianism, one that seeks to reformulate the public sphere according to private sphere practices. Retaining their participatory and experimental character, they continue to act as prefigurative spaces in which new, solidary socio-economic relationships are intentionally fostered and effectively concretized, both within the community and even beyond it, as evidenced in the PTDC's institutional partnerships.

PTDC manager Anandi points to how these kinds of prefigurative institutions, which facilitate the concretization of Aurovilians' aspirations in everyday community life, are critical for manifesting Auroville as an enacted utopian community:

> 'I've seen here so much … goodwill. Where would that goodwill have been expressed if Pour Tous would not have been there? In the supermarket, getting a beer? So, not only you create a space where that can happen, it's also – *it invites*. And that, for me, is very important. If we don't create the space that calls for that, how are we expecting it to manifest? In a supermarket? That would be a real miracle!' (Interview with Anandi, PTDC manager, 14 April 2016)

However, it is important to underline again that many Aurovilians remain critical of their socio-economic achievements, as we saw in the case of the PTDC, because they consider them to be only partial and thus even hypocritical in light of the ideals they seek to prefigure. I draw on an observation by Arthur in reconciling these perceptions, which is that "in Sri Aurobindo's definition of a subjective society lies the key of Auroville".[50] Sri Aurobindo described a subjective society as an intermediary stage, a passage from a society governed by ego to one governed by the divine (gnostic society). In that transitional period, bound to be uncomfortable, people would invent tools, means and frameworks that would contain elements of both – as prefigurative of the gnostic society as possible, but still only approximating it.

Auroville and Beyond: The Grounded Hopes and Horizons of Spiritually Prefigurative Practice – A Conclusion

So what's the point of utopia?
The point is this: to keep walking.

Eduardo Galeano, 1993

Asking, we walk.

Zapatista slogan

This autoethnographic exploration of the development of Auroville offers a hopeful insight into the potential of a prefigurative articulation of utopian practice, one in which utopian ideals engage with present conditions in a flexible and reflexive transformative process. Among the key contributions gained from observing this unique project is the revelation that a spiritual quest can underly, strategically articulate and sustain a prefigurative utopian project. The community is not conceptually or practically dissociated from the challenges (and potentialities) of the conditions in which it is embedded – social, political, economic and environmental – but predicates itself on the incorporation of these challenges by virtue of a spiritual world view that seeks out their transformation. I find that the lens of prefiguration is particularly adapted to understanding this world view and the utopian practice that arises from it given that it is not a fixed utopian vision of the future but an evolutionary process to be engaged through praxis – an experience that may be shared by other spiritual or a-spiritual groups.

Davina Cooper (2017) highlights that prefigurative conceptualization, just like prefigurative practice, must be both reflexive and provisional. Each are key to an ongoing, evolutionary praxis of utopianism – particularly in an established 'alternative' society such as Auroville, whose experimental nature risks waning over time – because they enable such praxis to be engaged in a learning process. This process of learning – what *The Auroville Charter* describes as 'unending education' (The Mother, 1968) – is related not only to understanding what works or does not work in terms of the practical application of utopian ideals but also, as both the utopian philosopher Ernst Bloch and utopian social theorist Ruth Levitas have highlighted, to the very nature of utopianism itself. Bloch (1986: 3) described it as 'learning hope', Levitas (2013) as the education of desire for a better way of life and The Mother as a 'thirst for progress' (quoted in Satprem, 1981: 65). For The Mother, both the thirst and the progress were of a spiritual nature, which Ruth Levitas (2013: 13) suggests is central to utopianism itself: 'If Utopia is understood as the expression of the desire for a better way of being, then it is perhaps a (sometimes) secularised version of the spiritual quest.'

Given that Auroville is a uniquely well-established intentional community that has scaled over 50 years, significant points of consideration pertaining to the perpetuation of alternative constructions of society emerge. While the anarchist ethos and praxis that underlies many alternative movements and practices often explicitly resist trajectories of institutionalization, Auroville's experience with 'flexible institutionalisation' (Clarence-Smith and Monticelli, 2022) responds to important critiques and concerns regarding the capacity of radical experiments to establish and maintain viable societal alternatives. Proponents of such experiments, many of whom share anarchist sensibilities and may thus find Auroville's institutionalization to be problematic, must therefore give this aspect of Auroville's evolution due consideration. However, at the time of publishing of this book, there is also an acute crisis of co-optation of Auroville's internal organization and development by government-appointed officials. As mentioned earlier, this issue has been brought to India's courts, whose verdict will determine the scope for a prefigurative praxis of institutionalization in this project for decades to come.

In light of my research, I would argue that the institutionalization of Auroville does not necessarily have to counteract its prefiguratively utopian nature. Rather, it compels us to consider the revolutionary notion that establishing institutions may be part of a stage in the process of prefiguring an alternative society that ensures their perpetuation when this institutionalization retains a prefiguratively utopian character, that is, when its organization facilitates the social reproduction of desired alternative social relations and when it remains experimental and therefore flexible and responsive to evolution.

In Auroville, such institutionalization may even be prefigurative of an alternative (to the) state. As Sri Aurobindo said: 'The State is bound to act crudely. ... It is incapable of that free, harmonious ... varied action which is proper to organic groups' (quoted in Clouston, 2003). In 'Prefiguring the state', while Davina Cooper (2017: 337) recognizes that 'For many scholars, radical change cannot emerge from (or within) the state but only from "outside"; and it is the presence or potential for an outside which is key', she argues that there is room, alongside left-wing state critiques, for a 'prefigurative conceptualisation' of the state that 'reimagines what statehood could mean' and 'rejects a sharp distinction between states and other political governance formations' (Cooper, 2017: 339). Among the three features of a prefigurative state that she proposes is embeddedness in everyday relations, in which the roles of administrators and beneficiaries overlap and are entangled, enabling 'a multiplicity of informal junctures and networks', through which policies may be 'advanced, transformed, gutted, enabled and thwarted' (Cooper, 2017: 345) through a rhizomatic 'stretching out, activating, and incorporating' of members of a polity and their projects in a 'constantly evolving governmental form' (Cooper, 2017: 343–4).

I recognize Auroville's mode of governance within these descriptions. My autoethnographic research reveals that policies are proposed, criticized, protested, ignored, reworked and amended by overlapping groupings of community members virtually continuously. Importantly, this 'embedded' nature has remained unchallenged by a shift in political organization from a direct democratic format towards something more akin to a representative democratic model. The latter observation is an important one for a consideration of what modes of governance are able to embody features of a prefigurative state.

My observations regarding the 'subjectively objective' nature of Auroville's administrative praxis also contributes to Cooper's important exploratory conceptualization of a prefigurative state. Policies abound in the community's collective organization at present, pointing to a Weberian process of bureaucratization, the trappings of which Auroville is not immune to, notably, its formulaic nature. This limits the 'free', 'various' and therefore arguably prefigurative praxis of governance described by Sri Aurobindo (quoted in Clouston, 2003), whether in the context of a Residents' Assembly gathering, such as the selection process, or the decision making of an administrative group. Yet, in the 'subjectively objective' articulation of this bureaucratization enacted in Auroville – critical, flexible and responsive to subjective perceptions – as well as attempts to engage Auroville's ideals in doing so, lays prefigurative potential for an alternative practice of (and/ or to) state administration. Such practice would benefit from being not only evoked but also assessed within the community, so that the spiritually prefigurative potential it contains can be appraised, upheld and advanced – even, or perhaps especially, in the face of ongoing takeover of Auroville's internal governance by government-appointed officials.

In the face of both bureaucratization and, more recently, a government takeover, a case must continue to be made for continued experimentation – all the more convincing in light of the successful accounts of how small-scale experiments progressed to shaping Auroville's communal organization and society, and the significant hurdles that were overcome for such embeddedness to be achieved (including a previous attempt at a takeover).[1] I hope that newer generations of Aurovilians will be struck by the potential of such experimentation, even in their 'private' individual spheres, for prefiguring change in the 'public' collective sphere of Aurovilian society – precisely what Sargisson (2000: 11) would describe as 'transgressive' utopian practice. In familiarizing others with this process, I wish for this research to increase appreciation for its exacting nature and the significance of what has been achieved so far – and to embolden fellow community members to sustain it in the face of the challenges that they will encounter. Our power to evolve as a society lies in such engagement, and such evolution is the very raison d'être of Auroville; indeed, my autoethnographic (re-) encounter with this experiment defied my own expectations of how central its ideals and spiritual world view are to Aurovilians, and how this translates into practice. As I became aware of how challenging it was to engage in, maintain and carry forward this 'utopian' community project, I had a new, and incredulous, appreciation for all those who had participated in sustaining it in the face of many limitations over its more than 50-year history. I gained a much more complex and multifaceted understanding of the multiplicity of ways in which we Aurovilians attempt to prefigure these ideals in our community[2] (although I am certain that many oversights remain, and I look forward to continuing to deepen my experience of and within Auroville). While it is important to be aware of and address our shortcomings, I am also certain that recognizing and fostering the ways in which we enact and embody Auroville's ideals – regardless of the circumstances – will further empower our individual and collective capacity to do so. In the words of Sri Aurobindo (2012: 94): 'Take the psychic attitude; follow the straight sunlit path, with the Divine openly or secretly upbearing you – if secretly, he will yet show himself in good time, – do not insist on the hard, hampered, roundabout and difficult journey.'

As has been highlighted in this account, the unique, integral, spiritually prefigurative nature of utopian praxis in Auroville pervades all areas of community life and activity – from art to politics, and from economy to education. In this scholarly attempt at understanding this phenomenon, the concept of prefiguration acts as an analytical lens through which the nature of Auroville's utopian praxis is analysed, assessing whether and how its practices attempt to strategically embody, and thereby propel, an evolution towards the community's spiritual ideals, while also highlighting instances in which these ideals are wielded in dogmatic ways – a blueprinting approach that clashes with the predominantly prefigurative ethos of the community. In considering a wide breadth of practices as prefigurative, my work reclaims and builds on early scholarship of prefiguration that considered sociocultural practices enacted alongside political ones (such as decision making) to be a part of the prefigurative repertoire. More recently, the concept was almost exclusively employed in defining the political practice of left-wing social movements, but such exclusivity does not serve the ultimate goal of prefigurative politics, which is driven by a desire to live in a society governed by other ideals than those of mainstream capitalism. I come back to the question my father asked himself as a protestor in the early 1970s: what is the society we are going to build once we win the revolution? Only a broad base of prefiguratively utopian practice, driven by alternative ideals, can begin to unearth this from us: 'Asking, we walk' (Zapatista slogan).

Thankfully, scholarship on prefiguration is beginning to turn its attention to a range of alternative (if not utopian) practices, from everyday practices to ecotopian movements (Monticelli, 2022), while the significance of alternative societies is garnering scholarly attention (Martell, 2022). Recent scholarship has centred on alternatives in India, such as *Alternative Futures: India Unshackled* (Kothari and Joy, 2017), a collection of essays on present initiatives and the futuristic scenarios they prefigure – in areas as wide-ranging as environmental governance, industry, law, energy, agriculture, localization, markets, health, sexuality and gender, and education. This kind of scholarship enables these kindred practices to be collectivized and, as a result, empowered. The uniqueness of Auroville's spiritually prefigurative world view is its aspiration to uplift humankind as a whole, while engaging with the wide range of challenges of human society to transform and evolve from these. This enables it to engage with, relate to and contribute to a 'pluriverse' of transformative initiatives, both in India and beyond (Kothari et al, 2019; Kaul et al, 2022), while also seeking to serve the cause of 'humanity as a whole' (The Mother, 1968), as asserted in the *Auroville Charter*.

Afterword

These days are steeped in a desperate need for radical change in the opposite direction of the world's current trajectory. The 'profit before life' motto of global capitalist 'development' is destroying the planet and its human and non-human inhabitants. To unlock the present critical situation and bring about the possibility of transitioning from 'planet crisis' to 'planet hope' resides with those communities creating alternative practices for sustainable life at the grass roots. Critics of localized experiments of alternative forms of being and living in and beyond the capitalist world worry that experiments of holistic, democratic, ecological and cooperative practices will not change the structures, dynamics and powers that sustain global capitalism and its recurrent crises. However, Suryamayi Clarence-Smith's book tells us a different story.

Her autoethnography of Auroville tells us the story of one of the world's most extensive and most well-developed intentional communities. Auroville's *Charter* states that the community belongs to humanity as a whole, as a place for the flourishing of the human soul and body, bridging past and present. For the past 55 years, Auroville's inhabitants – several thousand, from all over the world – have been reinventing communal life, attaining exceptional levels of ecological restoration and reforestation, a cutting-edge practice of direct democracy, and a new economic model – all from a grass-roots search for real sustainability, beyond grand discourses. Learning about this experience and understanding what was achieved is vital for the needed change our world must work towards.

The impact of this book on our understanding of prefigurative praxis and utopia cannot be overemphasized. Three contributions come to mind. First, Clarence-Smith focuses on process. As she explains, she intended not to document the Auroville community's alternative practices but to investigate the complex processes by which these collective actions and their alternative practices emerge and are established. In addition to many deliberative, organizing and learning activities, praxis encompasses moments of contradiction and conflict. Navigating those contradictions and conflicts, both internal and external, is a component of prefigurative praxis. The second contribution is the clear distinction between abstract and concrete utopia.

The main difference between abstract and concrete utopia, writes Ernst Bloch, is that abstract utopia is a ready-made utopia, while concrete utopia is of an anticipatory kind that rejects both abstract utopian dreaminess and immature utopian socialism. As a concrete utopia, Auroville critiques the existing situation by prefiguring a different, not-yet reality. The Not Yet is a central notion in Bloch's philosophy, for he sees humanity as an unfinished project, a possibility and something to be discovered. The discovery, through the creation of concrete utopias, is praxis oriented. The third learning from the book is that spirituality is not a deterrent to radical change but a significant element of prefigurative praxis. This last insight emerges from the unique rootedness of Auroville in the Indian ashram tradition and speaks to the importance of including experiences of the Global South in exploring the concept and practice of utopia.

At the time of writing, Auroville is facing the challenge of defending itself from the authoritarian governmental imposition of a development agenda that is undoing and destroying the community achievements of a half-century. This turn of events is unspeakable but also unsurprising: every attempt to create an alternative to development is under the surveillance and potential attack of authoritarian governments and economic powers; in this case, it manifested as taking over democratic community institutions, destroying thousands of trees and seizing the community's lands and assets, ironically, in the name of 'development'.

To think that all was in vain would be a mistake. Hope must be disappointable, writes Bloch. Concrete utopias emerge from within the society that we need to criticize and change, not from outside it. Navigating the processes of creating concrete utopias is complex and uncertain, with no reassurance. Organizing hope opens in a forward direction, in a 'future-oriented direction', as Bloch claims. Hence, hope is not confidence; it is always in danger. However, since hope as praxis is embedded in the human venturing beyond to find a flourishing life, experiments like Auroville create excess. This surplus possibility cannot be taken away or translated into the language of power, the state, the law or policy. State translation of concrete utopias is always incomplete. What aspects of Auroville's prefigurative praxis remain untranslatable into the destructive logic of state power? In Clarence-Smith's beautiful autoethnography, we might find important clues to answer this question.

Ana Cecilia Dinerstein
Bristol
22 February 2023

A Dream
(The Mother, 1954)

There should be somewhere on earth a place which no nation could claim as its own, where all human beings of goodwill who have a sincere aspiration could live freely as citizens of the world and obey one single authority, that of the supreme Truth; a place of peace, concord and harmony where all the fighting instincts of man would be used exclusively to conquer the causes of his sufferings and miseries, to surmount his weaknesses and ignorance, to triumph over his limitations and incapacities; a place where the needs of the spirit and the concern for progress would take precedence over the satisfaction of desires and passions, the search for pleasure and material enjoyment. In this place, children would be able to grow and develop integrally without losing contact with their souls; education would be given not for passing examinations or obtaining certificates and posts but to enrich existing faculties and bring forth new ones. In this place, titles and positions would be replaced by opportunities to serve and organise; the bodily needs of each one would be equally provided for, and intellectual, moral and spiritual superiority would be expressed in the general organisation not by an increase in the pleasures and powers of life but by increased duties and responsibilities. Beauty in all its artistic forms, painting, sculpture, music, literature, would be equally accessible to all; the ability to share in the joy it brings would be limited only by the capacities of each one and not by social or financial position. For in this ideal place money would no longer be the sovereign lord; individual worth would have a far greater importance than that of material wealth and social standing. There, work would not be a way to earn one's living but a way to express oneself and to develop one's capacities and possibilities while being of service to the community as a whole, which, for its own part, would provide for each individual's subsistence and sphere of action. In short, it would be a place where human relationships, which are normally based almost exclusively on competition and strife, would be replaced by relationships of emulation in doing well, of collaboration and real brotherhood.

The earth is certainly not ready to realise such an ideal, for mankind does not yet possess sufficient knowledge to understand and adopt it nor the conscious force that is indispensable in order to execute it; that is why I call it a dream.

And yet this dream is in the course of becoming a reality; that is what we are striving for in Sri Aurobindo's Ashram, on a very small scale, in proportion to our limited means. The realisation is certainly far from perfect, but it is progressive; little by little we are advancing towards our goal which we hope we may one day be able to present to the world as a practical and effective way to emerge from the present chaos, to be born into a new life that is more harmonious and true.

APPENDIX B

The Auroville Charter
(The Mother, 1968)

1. Auroville belongs to nobody in particular. Auroville belongs to humanity as a whole. But, to live in Auroville, one must be a willing servitor of the divine consciousness.
2. Auroville will be the place of an unending education, of constant progress, and a youth that never ages.
3. Auroville wants to be the bridge between the past and the future. Taking advantage of all discoveries from without and from within, Auroville will boldly spring towards future realisations.
4. Auroville will be a site of material and spiritual researches for a living embodiment of an actual human unity.

To Be a True Aurovilian
(The Mother, 1971)

1. The first necessity is the inner discovery in order to know what one truly is behind social, moral, cultural, racial and hereditary appearances. At the centre there is a being free, vast and knowing, who awaits our discovery and who ought to become the active centre of our being and our life in Auroville.

2. One lives in Auroville in order to be free from moral and social conventions; but this freedom must not be a new slavery to the ego, to its desires and ambitions. The fulfilment of one's desires bars the way to the inner discovery which can only be achieved in the peace and transparency of perfect disinterestedness.

3. The Aurovilian should lose the sense of personal possession. For our passage in the material world, what is indispensable to our life and to our action is put at our disposal according to the place we must occupy. The more we are consciously in contact with our inner being, the more are the exact means given to us.

4. Work, even manual work, is something indispensable for the inner discovery. If one does not work, if one does not put his consciousness into matter, the latter will never develop. To let the consciousness organise a bit of matter by means of one's body is very good. To establish order around oneself helps to bring order within oneself. One should organise one's life not according to outer and artificial rules, but according to an organised inner consciousness, for if one lets life go on without subjecting it to the control of the higher consciousness, it becomes fickle and inexpressive. It is to waste one's time in the sense that matter remains without any conscious utilisation.

5. The whole earth must prepare itself for the advent of the new species, and Auroville wants to work consciously to hasten this advent.

6. Little by little it will be revealed to us what this new species must be, and meanwhile the best course is to consecrate oneself entirely to the Divine.

Notes

Chapter 1

1. Harris, 2009: 28.
2. For a biography of Sri Aurobindo, see Peter Heehs (2008). For a biography of The Mother, see Georges van Vrekhem (2000).
3. Personal communication, 18 October 2019.
4. Pseudonym.
5. Interview with Gandhimatti, 15 March 2018.
6. Interview with Gandhimatti, 15 March 2018.
7. All of Sri Aurobindo's works are accessible online at: https://incarnateword.in (accessed 14 April 2023).
8. Notable exceptions are Findhorn and Damanhur, who closely match Auroville in longevity and have also garnered significant recognition.
9. Examples of intentional communities that have faced moral and legal persecution include Rajneeshpuram and Oneida.
10. The Auroville Foundation is a statutory (autonomous) body registered under the Ministry of Education of the government of India (see: https://aurovillefoundation.org.in [accessed 14 April 2023]).
11. On Findhorn, see Kunze (2012) Sargisson (2000), Spielvogel (1985) and Sutcliffe (2000). On Damanhur, see Meijerink (2003), Pace (2000) and Metcalf (1999). On Auroville, a collection of research is available online at: www.aurorepo.in [accessed 25 April 2023].
12. A notable exception is Lucy Sargisson, who proposed the theoretical framework of 'transgressive utopianism' through which to understand the significance of alternative, individual and communal lifestyle practices in contemporary intentional communities (examined in detail in Chapter 2) (see Sargisson, 2000).
13. However, Robert Schehr and Marguerite Bouvard have highlighted the contributions of intentional communities to mainstream practices, for instance, in education, environment and social rights.
14. See the Awareness Through the Body website at: https://awarenessthroughthebody.org (accessed 14 April 2023).
15. See the Auroville Art Camp website at: https://aurovilleartcamp.wordpress.com (accessed 14 April 2023).

Chapter 2

1. Alternate terms used are 'communes', 'utopian communities', 'communal utopias', 'cooperative communities', 'ecovillages' and so on.
2. See: www.ic.org/directory/listings/ (accessed 14 April 2023).
3. Swami Vivekananda founded the Ramakrishna Math in 1866 – a monastic order in which monks live communally and focus on spiritual practices and on the dissemination

of Ramakrishna's and Vivekananda's teachings, through which a concurrent reform of Hinduism and Indian society was sought based on the revival and spread of Vedic wisdom – and the Ramakrishna Mission – a humanitarian voluntary organization in which monks and devotees engage in charitable work. Vivekananda travelled and educated audiences in India and abroad, establishing a network of Vedanta societies; today, the Ramakrishna Movement counts close to two hundred centres worldwide.

[4] However, in the early years, The Mother stated that there should be no use of drugs or alcohol in Auroville (see The Mother, 1977).

[5] Although another utopian communal experiment, Anandanagar, was undertaken by the Ananda Marga sect in Bengal (see Voix, 2011).

[6] Margaret Mead (1970) first wrote about 'prefigurative culture' in *Culture and Commitment: A Study of the Generation Gap*.

Chapter 3

Permission was granted by Peter Lang to reprint content from 'Auroville: an experiment in spiritually prefigurative utopian practice', a chapter by the same author (Suryamayi Aswini Clarence-Smith) published in *Transgressive Utopianism: Essays in Honor of Lucy Sargisson* (2021), edited by Raffaella Baccolini and Lyman Tower Sargent, in the Ralahine Utopian Studies Series (Volume 22). ISBN: 9781789978803.

[1] It is important here to note that there are no prescribed spiritual practices or protocols in Auroville; Integral Yoga is a fundamentally anarchist spirituality, in that it recognizes and affirms that each individual has a unique spiritual path and is sovereign in its discovery and enactment.

[2] There were 81 in total, corresponding to approximately a third of those eligible.

[3] Work seen as service towards something higher also has roots in religious traditions (see Sargisson, 2000: 88).

[4] The other two being Bhakti Yoga, or the yoga of devotion, and Jnana Yoga, or the yoga of spiritual and philosophical study.

Chapter 4

Permission was granted by Springer Nature to reprint content from 'Flexible institutionalisation in Auroville: a prefigurative alternative to development', an article co-authored by Suryamayi Aswini Clarence-Smith (the author of this monograph) and Lara Monticelli (the editor of the series in which this monograph appears), published in *Sustainability Science*, 17(2022), a special issue edited by F. Demaria, J. Gerber and B. Akbulut: 'Alternatives to sustainable development: what can we learn from concrete experiences?'

[1] The intervention of government-appointed administrators referred to took place in the period immediately preceding, and was ongoing at, the time of publication of this book.

[2] During the ten months I was carrying out fieldwork alone, this was the case for a number of significant policies – such as the 'Code of conduct' for Auroville's economic units (Auroville Foundation, 2017) and the new entry policy (amended in 2017) for the admission and termination of community membership – and the entire selection process for Auroville's working groups.

[3] A recently highlighted example of this is the case of Rajneeshpuram in Oregon, which was the subject of the Netflix documentary series *Wild Wild Country*.

[4] Past members include reputed academics like Professor Amartya Sen, directors-general of UNESCO and members of the Club of Rome (see Auroville, 2021b).

[5] The secretary of the Auroville Foundation is the highest position within the Auroville Foundation Office (AVFO).

[6] Notable grants have been made by RAMCO, in Auroville's education and ecological sector, and NLC India Limited, towards infrastructure (an access road to the Auroville Visitors Centre).

[7] At present, the working groups that are directly accountable to the Auroville Foundation are the Working Committee, the FAMC and the ATDC.

[8] The Working Committee, Auroville Council, the ATDC and the FAMC.

[9] The FAMC in 2016, and the ATDC in 2017.

[10] Conversation with Chintan Kella, visiting researcher to Auroville, 30 December 2017.

[11] This decision-making process can be fast-tracked in the case of emergency topics, in which case, there is no feedback process: a proposal is presented to the community and immediately passes to a vote.

[12] Personal communication to the author by Olivier Barot, 2 February 2023.

[13] While horizontal decision making has been used to organize thousands of participants in direct action social movements, such as Occupy Wall Street and the Global Justice Movement, the Auroville community's scope of enactment is much broader and long-lasting than that of organizing direct actions.

Chapter 5

Permission was granted by Wiley to reprint content from 'Prompting spiritually prefigurative practice: collective decision-making in Auroville, India', a chapter by the same author (Suryamayi Aswini Clarence-Smith) published in *Eco-communities: Surviving Well Together* (2023), edited by Jenny Pickerill, in The Antipode Book Series.

[1] This was during my doctoral fieldwork period.

[2] These were introduced to the Auroville Council by a visiting collective intelligence researcher, Jean-François Noubel.

Chapter 6

[1] The Yoga of Action, one of the three main yoga *margas* ('paths of yoga').

[2] Written in 1954, before Auroville was founded, it makes reference to the Sri Aurobindo Ashram but is prefigurative of what would emerge as the Auroville project.

[3] 'Kind' is meant here in the sense of material offerings.

[4] The Sri Aurobindo Society is a not-for-profit institution The Mother founded in 1960. She was its president until her passing in 1973, after which the Sri Aurobindo Society and the Auroville community's relationship became challenging, ultimately resulting in government intervention and the establishment of Auroville as a foundation independent from the Sri Aurobindo Society.

[5] Not to be confused with what is termed the 'Maintenance system', which refers specifically to the system of allocation of stipends to community members, the 'Auroville Maintenance Fund' is the name of an Auroville-administered fund that consists of multiple accounts of Aurovilian individuals, commercial units, community services and projects.

[6] In 1989, when this contribution was introduced, it was voluntary and amounted to Rs. 200 per individual. By 2018, this amount had increased to Rs. 3,150 per individual and was deducted from all individual Aurovilians, unless they had been granted a waiver.

[7] The question of what constitutes 'basic needs' is an ongoing debate, including in Auroville (see Streeten, 1984).

[8] The BCC was mandated in February 2006 and became a functional body in September 2008, structured as a representative group consisting of 12 members from different Auroville working groups and various 'sector groups' – one each from the ATDC, the Auroville Board of Commerce, the Auroville Board of Services, SAIIER (board of education), the Auroville Council, Green Group (Farm & Forest), Land Board, Unity

Fund, Project Coordination Group, Human Resources Team (in charge of community member Maintenances) and Guest Facilities Coordination Group, two members representing the 'community at large', and a secretary, resource person and chairman.

9   Interview with Otto, 26 October 2017.

10 It is important to note that already in the prior decade (the 1990s), communal budget managers, faced with budgetary constraints, had asked certain services (such as the Electrical Service) to charge Aurovilian consumers minimal amounts (below cost price) in order to replace a portion of Central Fund financing.

11 Personal communication from BCC member 'Nicole', 16 March 2015.

12 I was later (in 2020) selected and joined the team as a BCC member.

13 Interview with 'Alaya', 9 May 2016.

14 Commercial unit executives are not a homogeneous group that shares the same views – I draw this particular observation from my attendance of Auroville Board of Commerce meetings during my doctoral fieldwork period.

15 Interview with 'Alaya', 9 May 2016.

16 Interview with 'Alaya', 9 May 2016. The actual BCC contribution policy requires units to contribute a minimum of 33 per cent of the profit of the previous year, not an amount determined on the basis of the contribution of the preceding year.

17 Interview with 'Alaya', 9 May 2016.

18 Fieldnotes from BCC meeting, 24 August 2017.

19 All names of BCC members used here are pseudonyms. I attended the meeting as an observer.

20 Rs. 3.6 crores is approximately GBP400,000.

21 The previous name for the allocating body of the communal fund (now the BCC).

22 Interview with 'Alaya', 9 May 2016.

23 All names of BCC members and the services they discuss are pseudonyms.

24 In 2017/18, my fieldwork research period, the total Maintenance amount was Rs. 14,880, with a cash portion of Rs. 11,000. Several people pointed out to me that it is below the Indian minimum wage; cross-checking in 2018/19, I found that it is only lower than Kerala's, the Indian state with the highest minimum wage, but the point remains valid – although this does not account for the provisions made by community services.

25 However, many Auroville services and eateries do not accept cash but, rather, only payment via the Financial Service, so as to serve exclusively members or registered visitors of the community, to whom the Financial Service issues 'Aurocards', its own debit card.

26 All categories of City Services Maintenance are standardized, whereas Commercial Unit Maintenances are not, though there is a cap on the amount that can be disbursed as a Maintenance *and* deducted as an expense (amounting to the standard Full-Time City Services Maintenance + the individual city services contribution amount).

27 I was approached by an FAMC member to assist in this during the course of my PhD.

28 Interview with 'Arthur', Aurovilian, 29 November 2017.

29 It is worth mentioning that a 'Work, maintenance & contribution policy proposal' published by the BCC in August 2010 suggested a 'flexible maintenance' stipulating 'People who have a high commitment and a real need may receive more than the minimum full-time maintenance' (see BCC, 2010).

Chapter 7

Permission was granted by Springer Nature to reprint content from 'Flexible institutionalisation in Auroville: a prefigurative alternative to development', an article co-authored by Suryamayi Aswini Clarence-Smith (the author of this monograph) and Lara Monticelli (the editor of the series in which this monograph appears), published in *Sustainability Science*, 17 (2022), a special issue edited by F. Demaria, J. Gerber and B. Akbulut: 'Alternatives to sustainable development: what can we learn from concrete experiences?'

[1] Interview with Otto, member of Seed, 26 October 2017.

[2] Interview with Otto, member of Seed, 26 October 2017.

[3] 'Arthur' is a pseudonym.

[4] Interview with 'Rebecca', member of Maheswari Circle, 4 December 2017.

[5] Interview with 'Rebecca', member of Maheswari Circle, 4 December 2017.

[6] Interview with Otto, member of Seed, 26 October 2017.

[7] Interview with Otto, member of Seed, 26 October 2017.

[8] Interview with 'Rebecca', member of Maheswari Circle, 4 December 2017.

[9] 'Rebecca' is a pseudonym.

[10] Interview with 'Rebecca', member of Maheswari Circle, 4 December 2017.

[11] Interview with 'Rebecca', member of Maheswari Circle, 4 December 2017.

[12] Interview with 'Siobhan', member of New Dawn Circle, 6 December 2017.

[13] 'Siobhan' is a pseudonym.

[14] Interview with 'Siobhan', member of New Dawn Circle, 6 December 2017.

[15] The standard monthly amount stood at Rs. 150 in 2018.

[16] It should be noted, however, that the question of what constitutes 'basic needs' in the Auroville community has not been collectively explored.

[17] Sri Aurobindo used the term 'subjective' to describe an experience or perception that was elicited from individuals' contact with a higher plane of consciousness (see Sri Aurobindo, 2014: 21–3).

[18] Interview with 'Arthur', 29 November 2017.

[19] The GST, a comprehensive consumption tax (collected at the point of purchase) on goods and services, introduced in India in July 2017, increased the prices of these by up to 28 per cent.

[20] Interview with 'Arthur', 29 November 2017.

[21] Interview with 'Anandi', PTDC manager, 14 April 2016.

[22] The main residential area (Aspiration) at the time of its founding.

[23] Interview with 'Anandi', PTDC manager, 14 April 2016.

[24] The BCC was called the 'Economy Group' at the time.

[25] Interview with Nicole, PTDC Support Group member, 12 April 2016.

[26] Interview with Joseba, former member of the Economy Group, 13 May 2016.

[27] Interview with 'Anandi', PTDC manager, 14 April 2016.

[28] Interview with 'Anandi', PTDC manager, 14 April 2016.

[29] Interview with 'Anandi', PTDC manager, 14 April 2016.

[30] A meeting of all community members that constitutes the ultimate mechanism of community decision making (on Auroville's political organization, see Chapter 4).

[31] Interview with Nicole, PTDC Support Group member, 12 April 2016.

[32] Interview with Nicole, PTDC Support Group member, 12 April 2016.

[33] Financed by the community's income-generating activities, community member contributions, government of India grants and foreign donations (see BCC, 2022).

[34] Interview with Nicole, PTDC Support Group member, 12 April 2016.

[35] 'Minimum' (Rs. 2,300 for adults; Rs. 1,200 for children), 'Medium' (Rs. 3,000 for adults) or 'Maximum' (Rs. 4,000 for adults; Rs. 2,000 for children). The standard contributions were calculated using the 'in-kind' value of the Auroville Maintenance as a basis, which covers a daily lunch at participating Auroville eateries. In 2016, the 'Medium' PTDC contribution of Rs. 3,000, represented 2.5 times the value of the in-kind lunch scheme (Rs. 1,200), equivalent to two-and-a-half meals per day.

[36] Interview with 'Anandi', PTDC manager, 14 April 2016.

37   This cost is the same as the PTDC's price of purchase given that the operational expenses of the service are subsidized by the Central Fund.

38   The PTDC support group consists of the service's founders, managers and engaged participants.

39   However, it is important to note that in a 2016 survey of all food outlets in Auroville, 71 per cent answered that their 'main' reason for going to the PTDC was 'Aspiration and Principles' (see Auroville Residents Assembly Service, 2016).

40   Conversation with Nicole, 5 October 2017.

41   Interview with 'A', PTDC participant, 16 May 2016.

42   Interview with 'D', PTDC participant, 30 April 2016; personal communication from 'S', PTDC participant, 12 May 2016.

43   Interview with 'Arthur', 29 November 2017.

44   Interview with Chali, PTDC participant, 21 May 2016.

45   Personal communication from 'SA', PTDC participant, 11 May 2016.

46   Interview with 'Anandi', PTDC manager, 14 April 2016.

47   Interview with Paul and Laura, executives of Maroma, a cost-price contributing unit to the PTDC, 9 May 2016.

48   Interview with Margarita, PTDC participant and executive of MG Ecoduties, a cost-price contributing unit to the PTDC, 27 April 2016.

49   Interview with 'Anandi', PTDC manager, 14 April 2016. Some PTDC participants already have their contribution allocated to the cooperative from the cash and/or in-kind portion of their Maintenance before the latter is disbursed to their individual accounts.

50   Interview with 'Arthur', 29 November 2017.

Chapter 8

1   On the previous attempt at a takeover, by the Sri Aurobindo Society, see Chapter 4.

2   I also believe that we would be enriched by research into how individual Aurovilians in various demographic groupings relate to, and embody, our ideals – beyond our previously prevalent focus on Auroville's pioneers (see Cebron, 2019; Devin, 2008) and the growing interest in generations raised in Auroville (Clarence-Smith and Tewari, 2016; Auroville Video Productions, 2011).

References

Aggarwal, A., L. Branagan, S. Clarence-Smith and H. Eveleigh (2021) *Auroville Citizens' Assembly Pilot: Exploring the Potential of Randomly Selected Community Members in Collective Decision-Making*. Auroville: Auroville Citizens' Assembly Exploration Team.

Aggarwal, A., S. Clarence-Smith, H. Eveleigh and A. Herbert (2022) *Dreamweaving the Auroville Crown 2022*. Auroville: Dreamweaving and Citizens' Assembly teams.

Anderson, L. (2006) 'Analytic autoethnography', *Journal of Contemporary Ethnography*, 35(4): 373–95. Available at: https://doi.org/10.1177/08912 41605280449 (accessed 14 April 2023).

Antiuniversity Now (2017) 'Cooperate or die', workshop. Available at: https://www.antiuniversity.org/archive/ (accessed 25 April 2023).

Auroville (no date) 'The Galaxy concept of the city'. Available at: www.auroville.org/contents/691 (accessed 23 January 2023).

Auroville (2014) 'Ilaignarkal Education Centre for Auroville workers of all ages and their wards, providing essential life skills'. Available at: https://auroville.org/page/ilaignarkal-education-centre-for-auroville-workers-of-all-ages-and-their-wards-providing-essential-life-skills (accessed 23 January 2023).

Auroville (2015) 'Organisational history and involvement of government of India'. Available at: www.auroville.org/contents/850 (accessed 23 January 2023).

Auroville (2016) 'SAIIER: Sri Aurobindo International Institute of Educational Research'. Available at: https://auroville.org/page/saiier-sri-aurobindo-international-institute-of-educational-research (accessed 23 January 2023).

Auroville (2017) 'Industry, commerce, money and economy'. Available at: www.auroville.org/contents/2825 (accessed 23 January 2023).

Auroville (2018) 'Financial Service/Auroville Maintenance Fund'. Available at: www.auroville.org/contents/2829 (accessed 23 January 2023).

Auroville (2020a) 'Statements of support from government of India'. Available at: www.auroville.org/contents/870 (accessed 23 January 2023).

Auroville (2020b) 'Auroville in brief'. Available at: www.auroville.org/conte nts/95 (accessed 23 January 2023).

Auroville (2021a) 'Awards'. Available at: www.auroville.org/contents/884 (accessed 23 January 2023).

Auroville (2021b) 'The International Advisory Council'. Available at: www. auroville.org/contents/1212 (accessed 23 January 2023).

Auroville (2022a) 'Census December 2022: Auroville population'. Available at: www.auroville.org/contents/3329 (accessed 23 January 2023).

Auroville (2022b) 'Statements of support: UNESCO'. Available at: www. auroville.org/contents/538 (accessed 23 January 2023).

Auroville (2022c) 'The Auroville Foundation'. Available at: www.auroville. org/contents/572 (accessed 23 January 2023).

Auroville Arts Service (2019) '1 minute video for Janaka from Centre d'art: LA CARAVANE INTERIEURE'. Available at: www.instagram. com/p/B3CEkE1F6p6/?igshid=9uynnl3aqmre&fbclid=IwAR3hH8Ev VNMnEzJK7LreOTjDiQiNct0qJDBVvTsEA5UTen1o2HFfA4fqUZ8 (accessed 23 January 2023).

Auroville Foundation (2001) 'Auroville universal township master plan: perspective 2025'. Available at: www.auroville.info/ACUR/masterp lan/index.htm (accessed 23 January 2023).

Auroville Foundation (2017) 'Code of conduct for all trusts and units of the Auroville Foundation'. Available at: https://wiki.auroville.org.in/wiki/ Code_of_Conduct_(CoC) (accessed 22 May 2023).

Auroville Media Liaison (2022) 'Auroville media kit'. Available at: https:// auroville.media/press/ (accessed 23 January 2023).

Auroville Radio (2017a) 'CAT12: progressive economy'. Available at: www. aurovilleradio.org/cat12-progressive-economy/ (accessed 23 January 2023).

Auroville Radio (2017b) 'The Auroville Foundation Act'. Available at: www.aurovilleradio.org/the-auroville-foundation-act/ (accessed 23 January 2023).

Auroville Radio (2018) 'Auroville internal consumption and production'. Available at: www.aurovilleradio.org/transitioning-towards-a-basic-needs-gift-economy-2/ (accessed 23 January 2023).

Auroville Residents Assembly Service (2016) 'Food distribution survey – results'. Available at: https://auroville.org.in/article/55767 (accessed 25 April 2023).

Auroville Video Productions (2011) 'The children of Auroville: part two, here and now'. Available at: Auroville Digital Archives.

Ayer, S., H. Sampath, M. Scherfler, M. Chakrabarti, V. Devatha, I. Gandhiprasad, M. et al (2021) *Report of the Study to Identify Auroville's Development Priorities for 2021–2026 (Draft)*. Auroville: L'Avenir d'Auroville – Town Development Council.

BCC (Budget Coordination Committee) (2010) 'Work, maintenance & contribution policy proposal', *Auronet*. Available at: https://auroville.org.in/article/23597 (accessed 14 April 2023).

BCC (2022) 'Auroville city services report (FY 2021–2022)'. Available at: https://budget.auroville.services (accessed 23 January 2023).

Berggreen-Claussen, M. (2020) 'Learning from the intangible: how can learning based on the three pedagogical principles of Integral Education be assessed?', MA thesis, University of Umea, Sweden.

Berila, B. (2016) *Integrating Mindfulness into Anti-oppression Pedagogy: Social Justice in Higher Education*. New York: Routledge.

Bernard, A. (2010) *Genesis of the Auroville Foundation Act*. Auroville: Auroville Press.

Birchall, J. (1997) *The International Cooperative Movement*. Manchester: Manchester University Press.

Blanchflower, P. (2005) 'Restoration of the tropical dry evergreen forest of peninsular India', *Biodiversity*, 6(3): 17–24.

Bloch, E. (1986) *The Principle of Hope* (Vol 1). Oxford: Basil Blackwell.

Boggs, C. (1977) 'Marxism, prefigurative communism and the problem of workers' control', *Radical America*, 6: 99–122.

Bouvard, M. (1975) *The Intentional Community Movement: Building a New Moral World*. New York: Kennikat Press.

Bregman, R. (2016) *Utopia for Realists: The Case for a Universal Basic Income, Open Borders and a 15-Hour Workweek*. Netherlands: The Correspondent.

Breines, W. (1989) *Community and Organization in the New Left 1962–68: The Great Refusal*. New Brunswick, NJ: Rutgers University Press.

Brown, M.A. (2016) 'Mauna Kea: Ho'omana Hawai'i and protecting the sacred', *Journal for the Study of Religion, Nature & Culture*, 10(2): 150–69.

Brown, S.L. (ed) (2002) *Intentional Community: An Anthropological Perspective*. Albany, NY: State University of New York Press.

Caldwell, S. (2001) 'The heart of the secret: a personal and scholarly encounter with Shakta Tantrism in Siddha yoga', *Nova Religio*, 5(1): 9–51. Available at: http://doi.org/10.1525/nr.2001.5.1.9 (accessed 14 April 2023).

Carson, R. (1962) *Silent Spring*. Boston: Houghton Mifflin.

Cebron, F. (2019) 'The Mother: an inner story by Auroville pioneers', documentary series. Available at: https://vimeo.com/user3896456 (accessed 25 April 2023).

Chang, H. (2008) *Autoethnography as Method*. Walnut Creek, CA: Berg.

Chari, A. (2016) 'The political potential of mindful embodiment', *New Political Science*, 38(2): 226–40. Available at: http://doi.org/10.1080/07393148.2016.1153192 (accessed 14 April 2023).

Cheater, A.P. (1987) 'Anthropologist as citizen: the diffracted self?', in A. Jackson (ed) *Anthropology at Home*. London: Tavistock, pp 164–79.

Clarence-Smith, S. (2015) 'Auroville: a practical experiment in utopian society', BA thesis, University of California, Berkeley, USA.

Clarence-Smith, S. (2016) 'PTDC: Auroville's communal cooperative as participatory platform of conscious citizenship'. Available at: https://aurorepo.in/id/eprint/3/ (accessed 25 April 2023).

Clarence-Smith, S. (2019a) 'Towards a spiritualised society: Auroville, an experiment in spiritually prefigurative utopianism', PhD thesis, University of Sussex, UK.

Clarence-Smith, S. (2019b) 'Auroville, a site of unending education', *Auroville Today*, Issue No. 359.

Clarence-Smith, S. (2021) 'Auroville: an experiment in spiritually prefigurative Utopian practice', in R. Baccolini and L.T. Sargent (eds) *Transgressive Utopianism: Essays in Honour of Lucy Sargisson*. Oxford and New York: Peter Lang, pp 139–58.

Clarence-Smith, S. (2022) 'Prefiguration and Utopia: the Auroville experiment', in L. Monticelli (ed) *The Future is Now: An Introduction to Prefigurative Politics*. Bristol: Bristol University Press, pp 154–68.

Clarence-Smith, S. and D. Tewari (2016) 'Auroville education survey, 1968–2013'. Available at: https://aurorepo.in/id/eprint/204/ (accessed 25 April 2023).

Clarence-Smith, S. and L. Monticelli (2022) 'Flexible institutionalisation in Auroville: a prefigurative alternative to development?', *Sustainability Science* 17(4): 1171–82.

Clarence-Smith, S., A. Rosegger, J. Axer, C. Grinnel and D. Storey (2016) 'What is research in the context of Auroville?', survey (unpublished).

Clouston, D. (2003) 'How to govern Utopia', *Auroville Today*, Issue No. 301.

Cohen, A.P. (1989) *The Symbolic Construction of Community*. London: Routledge.

Cohen, A.P. (1992) 'Self-conscious anthropology', in J. Okely and H. Callaway (eds) *Anthropology and Autobiography*. London: Routledge, pp 155–68.

Connolly, W.E. (2002) *Neuropolitics: Thinking, Culture, Speed*. Minneapolis: University of Minnesota Press.

Cooper, D. (2017) 'Prefiguring the state', *Antipode*, 49(2): 335–56. Available at: https://doi.org/10.1111/anti.12277 (accessed 14 April 2023).

Cooper, D. (2020) 'Towards an adventurous institutional politics: the prefigurative "as if" and the reposing of what's real', *The Sociological Review*, 68(5): 893–916. Available at: https://doi.org/10.1177/0038026120915148 (accessed 14 April 2023).

Damanhur Foundation (no date) 'Damanhur: a door towards a new future'. Available at: https://damanhur.org (accessed 25 April 2023).

D'Andrea, A. (2007) 'Osho International Meditation Resort (Pune, 2000s): an anthropological analysis of Sannyasin therapies and the Rajneesh legacy', *Journal of Humanistic Psychology*, 47(1): 91–116. Available at: http://doi.org/10.1177/0022167806292997 (accessed 14 April 2023).

Datla, C. (2014) 'The constructive role of conflict in an intentional community: Auroville as a case-study', MSc thesis, Northeastern University, USA.

Davies, C.A. (2007) *Reflexive Ethnography: A Guide to Researching Selves and Others* (2nd edn). London: Routledge.

Davies, W. (2015) *The Happiness Industry: How the Government and Big Business Sold Us Well-Being*. London: Verso.

Decreus, T., M. Lievens and A. Braeckman (2014) 'Building collective identities: how new social movements try to overcome post-politics', *Parallax*, 20(2): 136–48.

Devin, C. (2008) *Turning Points: An Inner Story of the Beginnings of Auroville*. Auroville: Auroville Press.

Dinerstein, A.C. (2015) *The Politics of Autonomy in Latin America: The Art of Organising Hope*. Basingstoke: Palgrave McMillan.

Dinerstein, A.C. and S. Deneulin (2012) 'Hope movements: naming mobilization in a post-development world', *Development and Change*, 43(2): 585–602.

Elsa, E. (2019) 'Indian PM Modi meditates in a cave, pictures go viral', *Gulf News India*. Available at: https://gulfnews.com/world/asia/india/ind ian-pm-modi-meditates-in-a-cave-pictures-go-viral-1.64028532 (accessed 23 January 2023).

Engels, F. (1880) 'The development of utopian socialism', in F. Engels (ed) *Socialism: Utopian and Scientific*. Available at: https://www.marxists.org/ archive/marx/works/download/Engels_Socialism_Utopian_and_Scienti fic.pdf (accessed 25 April 2023).

Epstein, B. (1991) *Political Protest and Cultural Revolution*. Berkeley, CA: University of California Press.

Eveleigh, H. and M. Arumugam (2021) *Exploring Auroville's Capacity to Flourish*. SAIIER: Auroville.

Fanning, C. (2011) *For All/Pour Tous & the Early Years of Its Economic Development*. Auroville: Social Research Centre.

Farias, C. (2017) 'That's what friends are for: hospitality and affective bonds fostering collective empowerment in an intentional community', *Organisation Studies*, 38(5): 1–19. Available at: https://doi.org/10.1177/ 0170840616670437 (accessed 14 April 2023).

Findhorn Foundation (no date) 'The story of the Findhorn Foundation'. Available at: https://www.findhorn.org/about-us/findhorn-foundation- our-story/ (accessed 25 April 2023).

Flores, C.I. (2009) 'Integral yoga activism: an exploration of its foundational elements and practices', PhD thesis, California Institute of Integral Studies, USA.

Franks, B. (2003) 'The direct action ethic: from 59 upwards', *Anarchist Studies*, 11(1): 13–41.

Galeano, E. (1993) *Las Palabras Andantes*. Mexico City: Siglo XXI.

Gilmore, L. (2010) *Theater in a Crowded Fire: Ritual and Spirituality at Burning Man*. Berkeley, CA: University of California Press.

Global Ecovillage Network (no date) 'Home'. Available at: https://ecovill age.org (accessed 16 January 2023).

Goldman, M.S. (2009) 'Averting apocalypse at Rajneeshpuram', *Sociology of Religion*, 70(3): 311–27. Available at: http://doi.org/10.1093/socrel/srp 036 (accessed 14 April 2023).

Graeber, D. (2004) *Fragments of an Anarchist Anthropology*. Chicago: Prickly Paradigm.

Graeber, D. (2010) *Direct Action: An Ethnography*. Edinburgh: AK Press.

Graeber, D. (2013) *The Democracy Project: a History, a Crisis, a Movement*. London: Allen Lane.

Grinnell, C., J. Lung, R. Venet and D. Pages (2013) *Educational Practices & Opportunities for Adults in Auroville*. Auroville: SAIIER.

Guigan, G. (2018) *Auroville in Mother's Words*. Auroville: Auroville Press.

Gurkaya, C. (2018) 'L'Empowerment des femmes villageoises au sein des unités de travail à Auroville: les cas de Wellpaper et de Naturellement', MA thesis, École des Hautes Études en Sciences Sociales, France.

Haberman, D. and L. Stevenson (1998) *Ten Theories of Human Nature* (3rd edn). New York: Oxford University Press.

Hadnagy, P. (2005) *The Auroville Foundation Act and The Mother's Guidelines*. Pondicherry: All India Press.

Hahn, T.N. (1993) *Interbeing: Fourteen Guidelines for Engaged Buddhism*. Berkeley, CA: Parallax Press.

Hardin, G. (1968) 'The tragedy of the commons', *Science*, 162: 1243–8.

Hardt, M. and A. Negri (2017) *Assembly*. Oxford: Oxford University Press.

Harris, R. (2009) *Alchemies of the Night*. Auroville: Auroville Press.

Heehs, P. (2008) *The Lives of Sri Aurobindo*. New York: Columbia University Press.

Herbert, A. (2017) 'Humanscapes', *Auroville Today*, Issue No. 340.

Horassius, M. (2013) 'Ethnographie d'une Utopie, l'exemple de la Communauté Internationale d'Auroville', MA thesis, École des Hautes Études en Sciences Sociales, France.

Horassius, M. (2021) 'Ethnographie d'une utopie: Auroville, cité internationale en Inde du Sud', PhD thesis, Écoles des Hautes Études en Sciences Sociales, France.

Johnson, G. and S.E. Kraft (2018) 'Standing Rock religion(s)', *Numen*, 65(5–6): 499–530. Available at: https://doi.org/10.1163/15685276-12341 510 (accessed 14 April 2023).

Jouhki, J. (2006) 'Imagining the other: orientalism and occidentalism in Tamil–European relations in South India', PhD thesis, University of Jyväskylä, Finland.

Juris, J.S. (2008) *Networking Futures: The Movements against Corporate Globalisation.* Durham, NC: Duke University Press.

Jzartl (2011) 'The Mother talks about total surrender', *YouTube.* Available at: www.youtube.com/watch?v=9PRa3Yx0mME (accessed 23 January 2023).

Kabat-Zinn, J. (2013) *Full Catastrophe Living: Using the Wisdom of Your Body and Mind to Face Stress, Pain, and Illness.* New York: Bantam Books.

Kanter, R.M. (1972) *Commitment and Community: Communes and Utopias in Sociological Perspective.* Cambridge, MA: Harvard University Press.

Kapur, A. (ed) (2018) *Auroville: Dream and Reality.* Gurugram: Penguin Random House India.

Kapur, A. (2021) *Better to Have Gone: Love, Death, and the Quest for Utopia in Auroville.* New York: Simon & Schuster.

Kateb, G. (1963) *Utopia and its Enemies.* New York: The Free Press of Glencoe.

Kaul, S., B. Akbulut, F. Demaria and J. Gerber (eds) (2022) 'Alternatives to sustainable development: what can we learn from the pluriverse in practice?', *Sustainability Science,* 17(4): 1149–58.

King, S.B. (2009) *Socially Engaged Buddhism.* Honolulu: University of Hawaii Press.

Khare, J. and C. Devin (2012) *Tell Me, My Friend: What is this Auroville?* Auroville: Auroville Press.

Klostermann, M. (1972) *Video Interview with Roger Anger.* Auroville: Auroville Digital Archives.

Kothari, A. and K.J. Joy (eds) (2017) *Alternative Futures: India Unshackled.* New Delhi: AuthorsUpFront.

Kothari, A., A. Salleh, A. Escobar, F. Demaria and A. Acosta (eds) (2019) *Pluriverse: A Post-Development Dictionary.* New Delhi: AuthorsUpFront.

Kunze, I. (2012) 'Social innovations for communal and ecological living: lessons from sustainability research and observations in intentional communities', *Communal Societies,* 32(1): 50–67.

Lamartine, A. de Prat de (1847) *Histoire des Girondins* (Vol 23). Brussels: Meline, Cans et Compagnie.

Latkin, C. (1991) 'From device to vice: social control and intergroup conflict at Rajneeshpuram', *Sociological Analysis,* 52(4): 363–77. Available at: http://doi.org/10.2307/3710852 (accessed 14 April 2023).

Leard, S. (1993) 'The routinization of charisma in a context of an inner-worldly mystic orientation', MA thesis, University of Saskatchewan, Canada.

Le Hunte, B., K. Ross, S. Clarence-Smith and A. Rosegger (2022) 'Lessons from utopia: reflections on peak transformative experiences in a university studio in Auroville, India', in A. Nicolaides, S. Eschenbacher, P. Buergelt, Y. Gilpin-Jackson, M. Welch, M. Misawa et al (eds) *Palgrave Handbook on Learning for Transformation,* New York: Palgrave Macmillan.

Levitas, R. (2011) *The Concept of Utopia*. Oxford: Peter Lang International Academic Publishers.

Levitas, R. (2013) *Utopia as Method: The Imaginary Reconstitution of Society*. London: Palgrave Macmillan.

Litfin, K.T. (2018) 'The contemplative pause: insights for teaching politics in turbulent times', *Journal of Political Science Education*, 16(1): 57–66. Available at: http://doi.org/10.1080/15512169.2018.1512869 (accessed 14 April 2023).

Madsen, O.J. (2015) *Optimizing the Self: Social Representations of Self-Help*. London: Routledge.

Maeckelbergh, M. (2009) *The Will of the Many: How the Alterglobalisation Movement is Changing the Face of Democracy*. London: Pluto.

Maeckelbergh, M. (2011) 'Doing is believing: prefiguration as strategic practice in the alterglobalisation movement', *Social Movement Studies*, 10(1): 1–20. Available at: http://doi.org/10.1080/14742837.2011.545223 (accessed 14 April 2023).

Majumdar, A. (2017) *Auroville: A City for the Future*. Gurugram: Harper Collins India.

Majumdar, A. (2018) 'Auroville: a test run for the future', TEDx Chennai, 11 March.

Martell, L. (2022) *Alternative Societies: For a Pluralist Socialism*. Bristol: Bristol University Press.

Marx, K. and F. Engels. (1848) 'Critical-utopian socialism and communism', in K. Marx and F. Engels (eds) *Manifesto of the Community Party*. Available at: https://www.marxists.org/archive/marx/works/1848/communist-manifesto/ch03.htm (accessed 25 April 2023)

Mascarenhas-Keyes, S. (1987) 'The native anthropologist: constraints and strategies in research', in A. Jackson (ed) *Anthropology at Home*. London: Tavistock, pp 180–95.

Mason, K. (2014) 'Becoming citizen green: prefigurative politics, autonomous geographies, and hoping against hope', *Environmental Politics*, 23(1): 140–58. Available at: http://dx.doi.org/10.1080/09644016.2013.775725 (accessed 14 April 2023).

Mazzucatto, M. (2013) *The Entrepreneurial State: Debunking Public vs. Private Sector Myths*. London and New York: Anthem Press.

Mazzucatto, M. (2018) 'Is the government more entrepreneurial than you think?', *Freakonomics Radio*, 5 September. Available at: http://freakonomics.com/podcast/mariana-mazzucato/ (accessed 23 January 2023).

Mead, M. (1970) *Culture and Commitment: A Study of the Generation Gap*. New York: Doubleday.

Mead, M. (1973a) 'Letter to whom it may concern', 30 October, Auroville Archives.

Mead, M. (1973b) 'Prefigurative cultures and unknown children', in P.K. Manning (ed) *Youth: Divergent Perspectives*. New York: John Wiley and Sons, pp 193–206.

Meier, J. (2006) 'Being Aurovilian: constructions of self, spirituality and India in an international community', *J@rgonia*, 4(10): 1–23.

Meijerink, E. (2003) 'The game of life: the significance of play in the commune of Damanhur', *Journal of Contemporary Religion*, 18(2): 155–68. Available at: http://doi.org/10.1080/1353790032000067491 (accessed 14 April 2023).

Metcalf, W.J. (1999) 'Damanhur: a "magical mystery tour"', *Communities*, 103: 17–20.

Minor, R. (1999) *The Religious, the Spiritual, and the Secular*. Albany, NY: State University of New York Press.

MiraAura (2002) 'Ashram departments'. Available at: www.miraura.org/aa/as/depts.html (accessed 23 January 2023).

Modi, N. (2018) 'PM Modi addresses programme to mark Golden Jubilee of Auroville'. Available at: www.narendramodi.in/pm-modi-addresses-progra mme-to-mark-golden-jubilee-of-auroville-foundation-539112 (accessed 23 January 2023).

Mohanty, B. (2008) 'Integral yoga: the spiritual ideals of Auroville', PhD thesis, California Institute of Integral Studies, USA.

Monticelli, L. (2018) 'Embodying alternatives to capitalism in the 21st century', *TripleC: Communication, Capitalism & Critique*, 16(2): 501–17. Available at: http://doi.org/10.31269/triplec.v16i2.1032 (accessed 14 April 2023).

Monticelli, L. (2022) *The Future is Now: An Introduction to Prefigurative Politics*. Bristol: Bristol University Press.

Mori, P.A. (2014) 'Community and cooperation: the evolution of cooperatives towards new models of citizens' democratic participation in public services provision', *Annals of Public and Cooperative Economics*, 85(3): 327–52.

Morton, T (2015) 'Buddhaphobia: nothingness and the fear of things', in M. Boon, E. Cazdyn and T. Morton (eds) *Nothing: Three Inquiries in Buddhism*. Chicago: University of Chicago Press, pp 185–265.

Mouffe, C. (2013) *Agonistics: Thinking the World Politically*. London: Verso.

Moylan, T. (1986) *Demand the Impossible: Science Fiction and the Utopian Imagination*. New York and London: Methuen.

Mukherjee, J.K. (1997) *Sri Aurobindo Ashram: Its Role, Responsibility, and Future Destiny: An Insider's Personal View*. Pondicherry: Sri Aurobindo International Centre of Education.

Namakkal, J. (2012) 'European dreams, Tamil land: Auroville and the paradox of a postcolonial utopia', *Journal for the Study of Radicalism*, 6(1): 59–88. Available at: http://dx.doi.org/10.1353/jsr.2012.0006 (accessed 14 April 2023).

Namakkal, J. (2021) *Unsettling Utopia the Making and Unmaking of French India*. New York: Columbia University Press.

New Indian Express (2022) 'Tamil youngsters' group holds meeting in Auroville to discuss Residents Assembly'. Available at: www.newindian express.com/states/tamil-nadu/2022/jun/16/tamil-youngsters-groupho lds-meeting-in-auroville-to-discussresidents-assembly-2466132.html (accessed 23 January 2023).

Nightingale, D. (2008) 'Catching the dream', *Ritam*, 5(1): 11–14.

North, P. (2014) 'Ten square miles surrounded by reality? Materialising alternative economies using local currencies', *Antipode*, 46(1): 246–65. Available at: http://doi.org/10.1111/anti.12039 (accessed 14 April 2023).

Noubel, J.F. (2013) 'The 6 agreements'. Available at: http://noubel.com/the-six-agreements/ (accessed 23 January 2023).

Okely, J. (1992) 'Participatory experience and embodied knowledge', in J. Okely and H. Callaway (eds) *Anthropology and Autobiography* (ASA Monographs Vol 29). London: Routledge, pp 10–28.

Okely, J. (1996) *Own or Other Culture*. London: Routledge.

Osborne, A. (1954) *Ramana Maharshi and the Path of Self-knowledge*. London: Rider.

Ostrom, E. (1990) *Governing the Commons: The Evolution of Institutions for Collective Action*. Cambridge: Cambridge University Press.

Pace, E. (2000) 'Damanhur, de la religion à la politique', *Ethnologie Française*, 30(4): 575–82.

Paden, R. (2002) 'Marx's critique of the utopian socialists', *Utopian Studies*, 13(2): 67–91. Available at: www.jstor.org/stable/20718467 (accessed 14 April 2023).

Paitandy, P. (2019) 'Let's talk trash', *The Hindu*. Available at: www.thehindu.com/life-and-style/fashion/lets-talk-trash/article26212023.ece (accessed 23 January 2023).

Pillai, S. (2005) 'Auroville: philosophy, performance and power in an intentional utopian community in South India', PhD thesis, New York University, USA.

Pitzer, D.E. (ed) (1997) *America's Communal Utopias*. Chapel Hill, NC: University of North Carolina Press.

Plato and J. Adam (1963) *The Republic of Plato, Volume 1*. Cambridge: Cambridge University Press.

Pohl, C. (2020) *Ever Slow Green*, documentary film. Auroville: Brainfever Media Productions.

Pommerening, M. (2017) 'Soul of sustainability? Inner dimensions of work for a sustainable society: an Auroville case study', MSc thesis, Medical School Berlin, Germany.

Prasad, N. (1965) *Life in Sri Aurobindo Ashram*. Pondicherry: Sri Aurobindo Ashram.

Protect Mauna Kea (no date) 'Home'. Available from: www.protectmauna kea.net (accessed 23 January 2023).

Queen, C.S. (ed) (2012) *Engaged Buddhism in the West*. Boston, MA: Wisdom Publications.

Queen, C.S. and S.B. King (eds) (1996) *Engaged Buddhism: Buddhist Liberation Movements in Asia*. Albany, NY: SUNY Press.

Raekstad, P. (2018) 'Revolutionary practice and prefigurative politics: a clarification and defense', *Constellations*, 25(3): 359–72. Available at: https://doi.org/10.1111/1467-8675.12319 (accessed 14 April 2023).

Reinhalther, J.P. (2014) 'Intentional communities: place-based articulations of social critique', MA thesis, University of Hawaii Manoa, USA.

Rimke, H.N. (2000) 'Governing citizens through self-help literature', *Cultural Studies*, 14(1): 61–78.

Rowe, J.K. (2015) 'Zen and the art of movement maintenance', *OpenDemocracy*. Available at: www.opendemocracy.net/en/transformation/zen-and-art-of-social-movement-maintenance/ (accessed 23 January 2003).

Rowe, J.K. (2016) 'Micropolitics and collective liberation: mind/body practice and left social movements', *New Political Science*, 38(2): 206–25. Available at: http://doi.org/10.1080/07393148.2016.1153191 (accessed 14 April 2023).

Rowe, J.K. and M. Carroll (2015) 'What the Left can learn from Occupy Wall Street', *Studies in Political Economy*, 96(1): 145–66. Available at: https://doi.org/10.1080/19187033.2015.11674941 (accessed 14 April 2023).

Roy (2014) 'The passage: on decision-making in Auroville'. Available at: www.auroville.org/contents/859 (accessed 23 January 2003).

Saari, A. and E. Harni (2016) 'Zen and the art of everything: governing spirituality in entrepreneurship education', *Ephemera: Theory & Politics in Organization*, 16(4): 99–119.

Sargent, L.T. (2010) *Utopianism: A Very Short Introduction*. Oxford: Oxford University Press.

Sargisson, L. (2000) *Utopian Bodies and the Politics of Transgression*. London and New York: Routledge.

Sargisson, L. and L.T. Sargent (2004) *Living in Utopia: New Zealand's Intentional Communities*. Aldershot and Burlington, VT: Ashgate Publishing Company.

Satprem (1981) *Mother's Agenda* (Vol 9). Paris: Institut de Recherches Évolutives.

Satprem (1985) *On the Way to Supermanhood*. New York: Institute for Evolutionary Research.

Schehr, R.C. (1997) *Dynamic Utopia: Establishing Intentional Communities as a New Social Movement*. Westport, CT: Bergin & Garvey.

Seidlitz, L. (2016) *Integral Yoga at Work*. Pondicherry: Indian Psychology Institute.

Seitz-Wald, A. (2013) 'Meet the "mindfulness caucus": politicians who meditate!', *Salon*, 10 July. Available at: https://www.salon.com/2013/07/10/meet_the_buddhist_caucus/ (accessed 25 April 2023).

Silver, A. (2022) *Learning from the Intangible*, documentary film. Auroville: The Learning Community.

Smucker, J.M. (2014) 'Can prefigurative politics replace political strategy?', *Berkeley Journal of Sociology*, 58: 74–82. Available at: https://berkeleyjournal.org/2014/10/07/can-prefigurative-politics-replace-political-strategy/ (accessed 25 April 2023).

Spicer, A. (2011) 'Guilty lives: the authenticity trap at work', *Ephemera: Theory & Politics in Organization*, 11(1): 46–62.

Spielvogel, J. (1985) 'Findhorn: the evolution of a spiritual utopian community', *The Journal of General Education*, 37(3): 231–44.

Sri Aurobindo (1908) 'Swaraj and the coming anarchy', *Bande Mataram*, 5 March.

Sri Aurobindo (1970) *The Life Divine – II*. Pondicherry: Sri Aurobindo Ashram.

Sri Aurobindo (1972) *Social and Political Thought*. Pondicherry: Sri Aurobindo Ashram.

Sri Aurobindo (1997) *The Human Cycle*. Pondicherry: Sri Aurobindo Ashram.

Sri Aurobindo (1999) *The Synthesis of Yoga – I*. Pondicherry: Sri Aurobindo Ashram.

Sri Aurobindo (2011) *Letters on Himself and the Ashram: Selected Letters on His Outer and Inner Life, His Path of Yoga and the Practice of Yoga in His Ashram*. Pondicherry: Sri Aurobindo Ashram.

Sri Aurobindo (2012) *The Mother with Letters on The Mother*. Pondicherry: Sri Aurobindo Ashram.

Sri Aurobindo (2014) *Letters on Yoga – III*. Pondicherry: Sri Aurobindo Ashram.

Sri Aurobindo (2015) *Essays on the Gita*. Pondicherry: Sri Aurobindo Ashram.

Sri Aurobindo Ashram (no date[a]) 'Departments of the Ashram'. Available at: www.sriaurobindoashram.org/ashram/departments.php (accessed 23 January 2023).

Sri Aurobindo Ashram (no date[b]) 'Sri Aurobindo on himself'. Available at: www.sriaurobindoashram.org/sriaurobindo/on_himself.php (accessed 23 January 2023).

Stand for Auroville Unity (no date) 'Home'. Available at: https://standforaurovilleunity.com (accessed 23 January 2023).

Streeck, W. (2016) *How Will Capitalism End? Essays on a Failing System*. London: Verso.

Streeten, P. (1984) 'Basic needs: some unsettled questions', *World Development*, 12(9): 973–8.

Study Group on Organisation (2016) '"Participatory working groups" & the 3-day selection process of their members'. Available at: https://auroville.org.in/article/58376 (accessed 25 April 2023).

Supreme Court of India (1982) *SP Mittal Etc. Etc vs Union of India and Others on Nov 8, 1982*. Available at: https://indiankanoon.org/doc/312 939/ (accessed 21 April 2023).

Sutcliffe, S. (2000) 'A colony of seekers: Findhorn in the 1990s', *Journal of Contemporary Religion*, 15(2): 215–31. Available at: http://doi.org/10.1080/ 13537900050005985 (accessed 14 April 2023).

Tanmaya (ed) (2014) *Sri Aurobindo and The Mother on Education: A New Education for a New Consciousness*. Pondicherry: Sri Aurobindo Ashram.

The Mother (1954) *A Dream*. Pondicherry: Sri Aurobindo Ashram.

The Mother (1968) *The Auroville Charter*. Pondicherry: Sri Aurobindo Ashram.

The Mother (1971) *To Be a True Aurovilian*. Pondicherry: Sri Aurobindo Ashram.

The Mother (1977) *The Mother on Auroville*. Pondicherry: Vak Trust.

The Mother (1998) *India the Mother*. New Delhi: The Mother's Institute of Research.

The Mother (2003a) 'Auroville', in Sri Aurobindo Ashram Trust (ed) *Words of The Mother – I*. Pondicherry: Sri Aurobindo Ashram Press, pp 187–348.

The Mother (2003b) *Words of The Mother – I*. Pondicherry: Sri Aurobindo Ashram Press.

The Mother (2003c) *Words of The Mother – III*. Pondicherry: Sri Aurobindo Ashram Press.

Thomas, H. and M. Thomas (2013) *Economics for People and Earth: The Auroville Case, 1968–2008*. Auroville: Social Research Center.

Tuhiwai Smith, L. (2012) *Decolonizing Methodologies: Research and Indigenous Peoples* (2nd edn). London and New York: Zed Books.

Udavi School (no date) 'Home'. Available at: https://udavi.weebly.com (accessed 23 January 2023).

UNESCO (United Nations Educational, Scientific and Cultural Organization) (2007) *Commemorative Activities for the 40th Anniversary of the Establishment of Auroville, an International Township*. Paris: UNESCO.

Urban, H.B. (1996) 'Zorba the Buddha: capitalism, charisma and the cult of Bhagwan Shree Rajneesh', *Religion*, 26(2): 161–82. Available at: http:// doi.org/10.1006/reli.1996.0013 (accessed 14 April 2023).

Van der Heyden, M.B. (2020) 'Towards human unity: realising conscious communication as development. Three case studies in Auroville, South India', MA thesis, The American University of Paris, France.

Van de Sande, M. (2015) 'Fighting with tools: prefiguration and radical politics in the twenty-first century', *Rethinking Marxism*, 27(2): 177–94. Available at: http://doi.org/10.1080/08935696.2015.1007791 (accessed 14 April 2023).

Van Vrekhem, G. (2000) *The Mother: The Story of Her Life*. New Delhi: Harper Collins.

Varshney, A. (2014) 'India's watershed vote: Hindu nationalism in power?', *Journal of Democracy*, 25(4): 34–45. Available at: https://doi.org/10.1353/jod.2014.0071 (accessed 14 April 2023).

Vidal, M. (2018) 'Manifesting the invisible', MA thesis, École des Hautes Études en Sciences Sociales, France.

Vidal, M. (2022) 'RA decision-making processes: past RADs, observations, ways forward'. Available at: https://auroville.org.in/article/90284 (accessed 23 January 2023).

Voix, R. (2011) 'Une utopie en pays Bengali: de l'idéologie sectaire hindoue à l'édification d'une alternative communautaire', in C. Clémentin-Ojha (ed) *Idées Religieuses, Engagement et Projets de Société en Asie du Sud Moderne et Contemporaine*. Paris: EFEO, pp 165–88.

Voloder, L. (2008) 'Autoethnographic challenges: confronting self, field and home', *The Australian Journal of Anthropology*, 19(1): 27–40. Available at: http://doi.org/10.1111/j.1835-9310.2008.tb00104.x (accessed 14 April 2023).

Warrier, M. (2003a) 'Guru choice and spiritual seeking in contemporary India', *International Journal of Hindu Studies*, 7(1–3): 31–54. Available at: http://doi.org/10.1007/s11407-003-0002-7 (accessed 14 April 2023).

Warrier, M. (2003b) 'Processes of secularization in contemporary India: guru faith in the Mata Amritanandamayi Mission', *Modern Asian Studies*, 37(1): 213–53. Available at: http://doi.org/10.1017/S0026749X03001070 (accessed 14 April 2023).

Watts, H. (2003) 'Research: large "R" or small?', *Ritam, The Bi-annual Auroville Journal*, 1(1): 14–16.

Weber, M., G. Roth and C. Wittich (1978) *Economy and Society: An Outline of Interpretive* Sociology (Vol 1). Berkeley, CA: University of California Press.

Wilde, O. (1891) 'The soul of man under socialism'. Available at: www.marxists.org/reference/archive/wilde-oscar/soul-man/ (accessed 23 January 2023).

Wilson, J. (2014) *Mindful America: The Mutual Transformation of Buddhist Meditation and American Culture*. Oxford: Oxford University Press.

Wright, E.O. (2010) *Envisioning Real Utopias*. London: Verso.

Writers for the 99% (2012) *Occupying Wall Street: The Inside Story of an Action that Changed America*. New York: OR Books.

Yang, L. and J. Willis (2017) *Awakening Together: The Spiritual Practice of Inclusivity and Community*. Somerville, MA: Wisdom Publications.

Yates, L. (2015) 'Rethinking prefiguration: alternatives, micropolitics and goals in social movements', *Social Movement Studies*, 14(1): 1–21. Available at: http://doi.org/10.1080/14742837.2013.870883 (accessed 14 April 2023).

Žižek, S. (2001) 'From Western Marxism to Western Buddhism', *Cabinet*, 2. Available at: www.cabinetmagazine.org/issues/2/western.php (accessed 14 April 2023).

Index